The First Franco-Americans

The First Franco-Americans

NEW ENGLAND LIFE HISTORIES FROM THE FEDERAL WRITERS' PROJECT 1938-1939

C. Stewart Doty

UNIVERSITY OF MAINE AT ORONO PRESS   Orono, Maine   1985

Copyright © 1985 by The University of Maine at Orono Press. All rights reserved. No part of this book may be reproduced, in whole or in part, by any means whatsoever, whether electronic, mechanical, photographic, or otherwise, without the express permission of the publisher in writing.

Manufactured in the United States of America by the University of Maine at Orono Printing Office.

First edition

9 8 7 6 5 4 3 2 1

ISBN 0-89101-062-9

For the Franco-American students
of the University of Maine;
that they might better know their heritage.

Contents

Introduction	1
Manchester, New Hampshire	11
Philippe Lemay	16
A Franco-American Grandmother	38
Henri Lemay	43
Old Town, Maine	47
Steve Comeau	52
Mr. and Mrs. Ovide Morin	58
David Morin, Brother of Ovide Morin	68
Mike Pelletier, Pulp and Paper Mill Worker	74
Alphonse Martin, Woodsman	88
Vital Martin	91
The Rev. Wilfred Ouellette	93
Alex Lavoie	97
William Green	99
Barre, Vermont	103
Stonecutter	107
Boardinghouse Keeper	109
Granite Worker	113
Stonecutters, Father and Son	115
Woonsocket, Rhode Island	119
Henry Boucher, Textile Worker	127
Afterword	143

List of Illustrations

Lawrence Morin (left) and his brother, Frank, pose in front of their first fruit stand. *From the collections of the Old Town Historical Museum.* — Front cover

Four boys at noontime in the Amoskeag Mfg. Company, Manchester, New Hampshire, May 1909. *Photograph by Lewis Hine. From the collections of the Library of Congress.* — 10

Fred Normandin (with bare arms) of 15 Bridge Street, Manchester, New Hampshire, with some of his friends. *Photograph by Lewis Hine. From the collections of the Library of Congress.* — 10

Mike and Catherine Pelletier, probably in the 1930's, and the accordions they entertained themselves and their friends with at home and at a variety of social occasions. *Photograph by Myers Studio; courtesy of Albert M. Pelletier.* — 46 (top)

The Morin brothers in front of their fruit store in Old Town, Maine in 1922.
From the collections of the Old Town Historical Museum.

46 (bottom)

The rafting grounds at Argyle Boom on the Penobscot River.
Reproduced from: Defebaugh, James Elliott. 1907. History of the lumbering industry of America, Volume 2. Chicago: The American Lumberman.

77

The Whitmore and Morse Granite Quarry in East Barre, Vermont.
F.S.A. photograph by Jack Delano. From the collections of the Library of Congress.

102

Two views of Woonsocket, Rhode Island, December 1940.
Both F.S.A. photographs by Jack Delano. From the collections of the Library of Congress.

121

Young boy leaves the Amoskeag Mfg. Company at quitting time (6:00 PM).
Photograph by Lewis Hine. From the collections of the Library of Congress.

143 and Back cover

The First Franco-Americans

Introduction

In the last half of the nineteenth century over half a million French speakers immigrated to New England from Quebec and Acadia. Surprisingly, we still know very little about their experiences in the new land.[1] Thanks to the census studies, we do have a good idea where these immigrants came from and where they settled.[2] Thanks to a series of community studies, we also know something of their efforts to found francophone parishes, schools, and newspapers.[3] Occasionally, we have even learned something about the connections between their ethnicity and their work life.[4] For the most part, however, these accounts either deal with Franco-Americans as an anonymous mass or they filter the Franco-American experience through the perceptions of New England francophone elites of priests, lawyers, doctors, and newspaper people. As a result, we are still unclear on how that first generation or so of ordinary Franco-Americans decided to come to America, to take the jobs they did, to get along in those jobs, to pick their life companions, and to deal with life's problems as they came. Recently, documentation has become available which at last gives us a glimpse into those matters.

This documentation consists of the life-history narratives recorded in the 1930s by workers of the Federal Writers' Project, a program of the New Deal's Works Progress Administration (WPA). At the time, several thousand ordinary Americans were interviewed, but few interviews came into print in those days. Instead, the great bulk of them were stuffed away in archives and warehouses. There they lay unused and forgotten. Only in 1980, thanks to Ann Banks' book, *First Person America*,[5] were readers at last introduced to a representative sample of these life-history narratives, and parts of two of the Franco-American narratives were included. By 1982, the entire collection became housed and inventoried in the Manuscript Division of the Library of Congress. Now, in this book, these earliest first-hand accounts of ordinary Franco-Americans are at last published. This book will also examine the circumstances which created these Franco-American life-history narratives and describe how they, with what we already know of New England Franco-Americans, give us a better understanding of the life experiences of those first Quebecois and Acadian immigrants to New England.

The Federal Writers' Project was not founded to collect life-histories of anyone.[6] Rather, its purpose was to provide work for unemployed writers. Many of the Project's alumni went on to distinguished literary and academic careers. Others were as ordinary as the people they interviewed. When the toilet overflowed in one Federal Writers' Project office, four writers, unemployed plumbers all, volunteered to fix it. The project writer who interviewed Old Town, Maine's Franco-Americans was an unemployed weaver in a local woolen mill. In short, the purpose was to provide jobless people with employment and income.

That did not mean, however, that any state director of the project wanted to be accused of overseeing intellectual leaf-raking. Rather, the Federal Writers' Project and each state director were determined to produce publishable work. Each state's initial goal was to research, write, and publish a guidebook of that state, modeled on the Baedeker guides. Without question, the project is most remembered today for those guidebooks, published commercially between 1937 and 1941. In preparing material for the history and cultural essays for the guides, the state offices collected a good deal of folklore, mostly of a traditional and rural nature. The Library of Congress materials of the Federal Writers' Project are full of Franco-American ghost stories, home remedies, devil and *loup garou* tales, recipes, an occasional community history, and an analysis of the Massachusetts Franch-language press. When folklorist Benjamin Botkin and sociologist Morton Royse were added to the project's staff in 1938, this collecting became more systematic and more focused on what was called the "living lore" of urban life and occupational histories, particularly that of ethnic Americans. Their influence led to the publication of *These Are Our Lives,* a collection of life-histories from the upper South's rural poor, and the ex-slave narratives in *Lay My Burden Down.*

One can see this progression from guidebook to "living lore" especially well in New England, where one would also most likely Franco-Americans. Frank Manuel, the New England director of the Federal Writers' Project and future French historian, was particularly attracted to the goals of Botkin and Royse and the desirability of doing publishable work. Already his workers had produced a commercially successful "instant book" on the New England hurricane of 1938. They were also engaged in book-length life-history projects similar to those of their southern counterparts. The "Living Lore in New England" project took life-histories from a number of ethnic groups. The "We Work in New England" project had people in all sorts of jobs describe their work experiences. The "Men Against Granite" project focused on that unique ethnic mix of Spanish, Italian, Scottish, and French Canadian granite workers in Barre, Vermont. All of these projects also produced life-histories of Franco-Americans.

One needs to keep in mind the nature and significance of these Franco-American life-history narratives. In the first place they are probably the earliest first-person accounts we have of ordinary Franco-Americans. Earlier Franco-American first-person accounts are almost exclusively limited to Franco-American male notables—priests, newspapermen, and members of the learned professions. More recently, thanks to the popularization of oral history, we have life-history narratives taken by Tamara Hareven's research team in Manchester, New Hampshire.[7] While those Franco-Americans interviewed by Hareven recall the early days of this century, they do so from the vantage point of the 1970s. In contrast, the Federal Writers' Projects' life-history narratives are simultaneously contemporary with the 1930s and push the collective memory back to the last of the 19th century.

Secondly, one needs to remember that these Franco-American life-history narratives were not taken by oral history professionals, using tape recorders. Rather than being trained professionals, the interviewers were local people who needed the work. They did get advice on how to interview. A typical list of instructions appears in *These Are Our Lives*.[8] It was easier if the interviewers knew their subjects. The Barre, Vermont interviews surely were made possible because interviewer Mari Tomasi had grown up in the neighborhood. In Manchester, interviewers Victoria Langlois and Louis Paré were fellow Franco-Americans. If one did not have that advantage, one could follow the advice of the Old Town interviewer:

> Some of the people I questioned seemed to be suspicious in spite of explanations in regard to the purpose of the work. They seemed to feel that the government had some hidden reason for wanting information about them. Maybe some of them objected to being considered as a "race apart," and preferred to be regarded as "just folks." A better atmosphere seemed to prevail when I left the French Canadian part out and told them I was looking up information for a book that would deal with life in Canada and Maine during a certain period. Just as much—and maybe more—information was forthcoming.[9]

Ann Banks spoke to enough surviving interviewers to get a good picture of how the interview process worked in an era before tape recorders. The interviewers first had to establish rapport with their subjects as they sat around a kitchen table or drank beer together. Some interviewers took notes. Others relied on memory. All learned to listen very carefully, not only to the stories being told but to the language patterns. This meant, of course, that each life-history was a collaborative effort between the interviewer and the person being interviewed. Each person's life was filtered through the concerns of the interviewer. In this way, these Franco-American life-histories vary one from another. The Old Town interviewer was more concerned with old time Old Town and its woods economy than he was with the Franco-American experience itself. Imminent death from silicosis seemed to hover over the interviews from Barre. Franco-American "success" dominated those done in Manchester. Yet, in spite of this filtering, the life-histories ring true.

Oddly enough, it is probably to our advantage that these life-histories were not published at the time of their creation. For one thing, interviewers frequently rendered accented English into a written dialect which sounds patronizing today. An earlier publication of New England Franco-American life-histories might have shared the same fate as those of the Cajuns. The Louisiana state director of the Federal Writers' Project reworked his state's folklore and life-history material into a book published by Houghton Mifflin in 1945. In his chapter on the Cajuns he felt obliged to quote not once, but twice, "I am a true man, me. I got credit at Fisher's Store; I got a share in my boat; and I make fourteen children for my wife."[10] Perhaps that was the voice of a typical Cajun in the 1930s, but perhaps it was not.

A second benefit of non-publication at the time is the fact that these life-histories come to us uncensored. The interviews coincided with widely publicized hearings by Congressman Martin Dies' House Un-American Activities Committee on charges that the Federal Writers' Project was a "Red nest." In such an atmosphere Frank Manuel took some alarm at the tone of the interviews with Barre granite workers. "For the time being we are not indulging in censorship," he wrote, "although we are conscious that this job will ultimately have to be performed."[11] Those interviews had a pronounced anti-management bias and those with Italian American workers, especially, more than a whiff of anarcho-syndicalism. By comparing the published life history narratives to the unpublished ones, it is clear that the latter ones come to us without being depoliticized and patronizing toward language and ethnicity.

Published now without condescension or censorship, these Franco-American life-history narratives speak for themselves as extremely rich and warm accounts of the human experience. They are more important than that, however. They also allow us to draw a composite view of the lives of ordinary Franco-

Americans from the Great Migration to the United States in the late nineteenth century to the Great Depression of the 1930s. This is especially true because the sample comes from representative Franco-American communities as varied as textile producing Woonsocket and Manchester, granite cutting Barre, and lumbering and papermaking Old Town.

Because each of those cities shaped its Franco-American citizens in special ways, the narratives which follow are arranged by those four cities. A historical introduction for each city provides a context for better understanding that city's narratives. The book will end with an essay on the ways these narratives have extended our knowledge of the life experience of ordinary Franco-Americans.

Some narratives in this book have been edited, while others appear in their original form. Narratives written in French-accented English seemed so patronizing toward Franco-Americans that they are rendered into standard English. Secondly, wherever possible the interviewer's voice was removed so that the narrative would remain in the first person. In every case, that required the deletion of a sentence here and there where an interviewer intruded into the narrative to make an introduction or to change the subject. The high literary quality of the Barre narratives, however, seemed to require the retention of the interviewer's voice. As a result, the Barre interviews remain in their original form except for changes in grammar.

Some narratives, however, required much heavier editing. In the William Green narrative several paragraphs on old-time food costs are deleted. Two versions each of the Mike Pelletier, David Morin, and Ovide Morin interviews were combined into one version each, with some material deleted and other material moved to advance the narrative flow and keep the finished narrative specific to the Franco-American experience. In their unedited form, these Old Town interviews, unlike the other narratives, were nothing more than field notes. On the other hand, the "field note" quality is sometimes particularly helpful. The Old Town interviewer frequently introduced his subjects with a description of their physical appearance and their homes. This material, again edited, is included in the book and allows the reader to visualize the subjects in ways sadly missing in the interviews from other cities.

For similar reasons, the Philippe Lemay narrative is several pages shorter than the original in accordance with the principle that second-hand knowledge should be removed from what should be a first-person account. Readers interested in his history of the Franco-American community of Manchester before his arrival and lists of early settlers and members of the French band might wish to consult the original in the Library of Congress. Some of the deleted material is included in the Manchester introduction. Several other paragraphs were re-ordered to make the first-person narrative flow more logically and chronologically. Rather than doing violence to the originals, this editing increases the power and eloquence of the life stories of Philippe Lemay and his fellow Franco-Americans from Old Town.

This is my first foray into the history of the French experience in North America. Trained as a historian of late-nineteenth and early twentieth century France, my intellectual journey across the Atlantic has incurred a number of debts. First, there is Marc Boucher, formerly of the Canadian-American Center of the University of Maine at Orono and presently a civil servant with the Quebec government. Thanks to his quiet persistence I became interested in studying the French of North America. He and Ronald Tallman, also of the Canadian-American Center, helped me gain research support from the Quebec and Canadian governments to develop my knowledge of French Canada's past. Secondly, in this step-by-step and not always easy development I have been regularly encouraged by my colleagues in the history department of the University of Maine at Orono, notably David C. Smith and William J. Baker. Other colleagues, historian Yves Frenette, folklorist Edward S. Ives, and Yvon Labbé, kindly read the manuscript and made helpful suggestions for revision. Finally, I thank Joseph Sullivan of the Manuscript Division of the Library of Congress for his generous assistance in locating these Franco-American materials in the Federal Writers' Project collection before they were inventoried and catalogued. The reader should also be aware that I am not a Franco-American. Thanks to my wife, my children are part Franco-American, but of the wrong sort. Their ancestor was a Quebecois fur trader in the American West.

NOTES

[1] Dyke Hendrickson, *Quiet Presence* (Portland, Me., 1980) is an excellent start toward such a history of Franco-Americans.

[2] Ralph D. Vicero, "Immigration of French Canadians to New England, 1840-1900," Ph.D. dissertation, University of Wisconsin, 1968; Albert Faucher, *Quebec en Amerique au XIXe siècle* (Montreal, 1973); Yolande Lavoie, *L'émigration des Canadiens aux Etats-Unis avant 1930* (Montreal, 1972).

[3] Pierre Anctil, "Aspects of Class Ideology in a New England Ethnic Minority: The Franco-Americans of Woonsocket, Rhode Island (1865-1929)," Ph.D. dissertation, New School for Social Research, 1979; Frances H. Early, "French-Canadian Beginnings in an American Community: Lowell, Massachusetts, 1868-1886," Ph.D. dissertation, Concordia University, 1979; Michael J. Guignard, "Ethnic Survival in a New England Mill Town: The Franco-Americans of Biddeford, Maine," Ph.D. dissertation, Syracuse University, 1976; Peter Haebler, "Habitants in Holyoke: The Development of French-Canadian Community in a Massachusetts City, 1865-1910," Ph.D. dissertation, University of New Hampshire, 1976; Philip T. Silvia, Jr., "The Spindle City: Labor, Politics and Religion in Fall River, Massachusetts, 1870-1905," Ph.D., dissertation, Fordham University, 1973; Richard S. Sorrell, "The Sentinelle Affair (1924-1929) and Militant Survivance: The Franco-American Experience in Woonsocket, Rhode Island," Ph.D. dissertation, State University of New York at Buffalo, 1975.

[4] Notably Tamara K. Hareven and Randolph Langenbach, *Amoskeag: Life and Work in an American Factory City* (New York, 1978); Hareven, *Family Time and Industrial Time* (Cambridge, 1982); Daniel J. Walkowitz, *Worker City, Company Town: Iron and Cotton Protest in Troy and Cohoes, New York, 1855-1884* (Urbana, 1978); and Gary Gerstle, "The Rise of Industrial Unionism, Ethnicity and Labor Organization in Woonsocket, Rhode Island, 1931-1934," Ph.D. dissertation, Harvard University, 1982.

[5] Ann Banks, *First Person America* (New York, 1980).

[6] In addition to Banks, pp. xi-xxv, the following account of the Federal Writers' Project is drawn from: Ray Allen Billington, "Government and the Arts: The WPA Experience," *American Quarterly*, XIII (1961), 466-479. Jerre Mangione, *The Dream and the Deal: The Federal Writers' Project, 1935-1943* (Boston, 1972); and Monty Noam Penkower, *The Federal Writers' Project: A Study in Government Patronage of the Arts* (Urbana, 1977).

[7] See especially: Studs Terkel, *Hard Times: An Oral History of The Great Depression* (New York, 1970) and Hareven and Langenbach, *Amoskeag*.

[8] William T. Couch (ed.), *These Are Our Lives* (Chapel Hill, N.C., 1939), pp. 417-421.

[9] Library of Congress, Manuscript Division, WPA Federal Writers' Project, Folklore Project-Life Histories (Cited hereafter as FWP/LH), Maine, note by Robert F. Grady, "Maine Living Lore, Old Town."

[10] Lyle Saxon, *et al.*, *Gumbo Ya-Ya* (Boston, 1945) pp. 179 and 206.

[11] Banks, p. xxii.

Four boys at noontime in the Amoskeag Mfg. Company. Manchester, New Hampshire, May 1909.

Fred Normandin (with bare arms) of 15 Bridge Street, Manchester, New Hampshire, with some of his friends. Fred had been working for the Amoskeag Mfg. Company for several months in 1909.

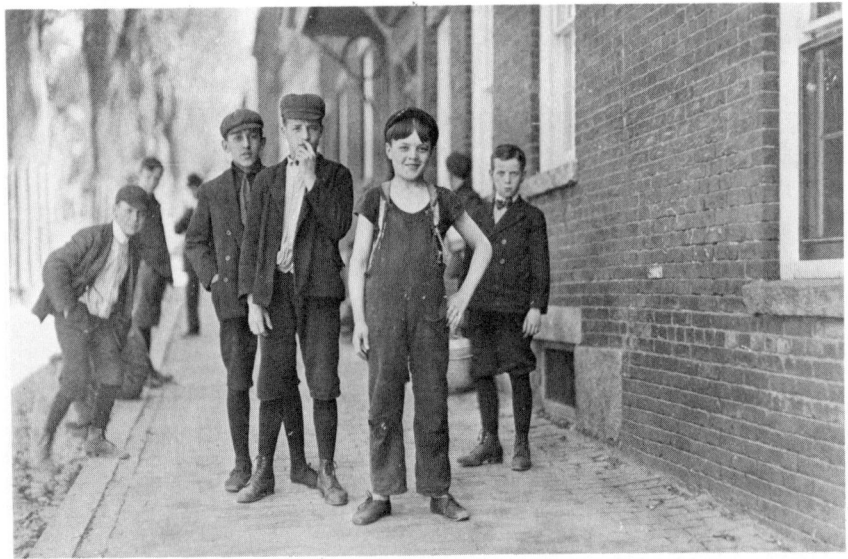

Manchester, New Hampshire

Viewed from the east, Manchester retains its turn-of-the-century appearance better than any other New England textile city. At a distance the mile-long multi-storied complex of brick factory buildings, so forlorn and derelict at close range, still seem to buzz with activity amid their complex of dams and canals along the Merrimack River. On the heights rising to the west of the river, stands the steeple of Ste. Marie's parish church and the *Petit Canada* which surrounds it. Up close, the well-kept tenements and houses of Manchester's Franco-American community still do buzz with activity. The people remain, but the factory which brought their ancestors to this place in the last hundred years is gone but for its shell. Yet, in its day, Manchester and the Amoskeag Manufacturing Co. seemed to epitomize the New England textile industry and its largely Franco-American work force.

Manchester and the Amoskeag were the creations of the Boston Associates, a group of Boston investers. In the 1820s, the Boston Associates began the Industrial Revolution in the United States by creating Lowell, Massachusetts, and its cotton textile industry. In the 1830s, the Boston Associates took what they learned at Lowell to create a more perfect version at Manchester, named this time not after a proper Bostonian but in honor of England's textile giant. The Boston Associates dammed the Amoskeag Falls, diverted its fifty foot drop through two parallel canals to power the textile factories, and purchased 15,000 surrounding acres. On those acres the Boston Associates built, by the early 1900s, a mile-long factory complex on one side of the river and a half-mile complex on the other. They surrounded the red brick factories with corporation housing, Spartan versions of New England townhouses to house the workers and managers at low rent. The other acres were sold off for private housing and business.

Manchester never became New England's largest textile city, but it was unique in several ways. By 1905, unlike anywhere else, all of Manchester's mills but one had come under the control of just one company—the Amoskeag Manufacturing Company. By 1922, the Amoskeag took over even that last one, to become the largest cotton factory in the world. That meant that the Amoskeag was Manchester, and Manchester was the Amoskeag. By early twentieth century, 17,000 of Manchester's 55,000 people worked for the Amoskeag. The only other large works were two shoe factories and a cigar manufacturer. Fifteen percent of the Amoskeag's workers lived in the company's corporation tenements. The others, if homeowners, bought or were given their house lots by the Amoskeag, which initially owned the city's real estate. In controlling the city's real estate, the Amoskeag controlled its development and, directly or indirectly, came to control the city's police force, politics, and business community.

Not only was Manchester a one-company city, that one company's offices were in another city, Boston. The officers of the absentee company seldom visited Manchester except through the reports of the agents they placed in charge there. Yet, in its entire history, the Amoskeag had only five agents, and three of them were three generations of the same family. This made for remarkable continuity of leadership, and in spite of the absentee control, generally progressive if paternalistic, management until World War I. Until then the agents maintained labor peace and enormous worker loyalty through an elaborate company welfare scheme of education, recreation, and housing.

Initially, as in Lowell, the Amoskeag mills and corporations housed Yankee mill-girls. By the Civil War, they had been replaced by lower-paid Irish immigrants. After the Civil War, they were supplanted by Franco-Americans from neighboring Quebec. By the end of the century entire French Canadian families would arrive daily from Quebec at Manchester's Boston and Maine Railway station. The rise of this Franco-American population can almost be traced by the increase in Franco-American parishes: St. Augustin in 1871, Ste. Marie in 1880, St. Georges and St. Antoine in the 1890s, and Sacre Coeur, St. Edmond de Pinardville, and St. Jean Baptiste in the next fifteen years. By the 1930s these parishes claimed a census of over 29,000, 38% of Manchester's total population and 35% of the Amoskeag's workforce.

In turn, these parish churches spawned French-language hospitals, orphanages, parish schools, and credit unions. In conjunction with them, the Franco-American community developed a number of fraternal and mutual benefit societies, notably the Société St. Jean-Baptiste and the Association Canado-Américaine, and a string of French-language newspapers.

As important as these institutions were, they were not nearly as central to the lives of the new Franco-Americans as the twin institutions of the family and the workplace. Moreover, as Tamara Hareven has told us, family and workplace were intimately linked. The plight of the rural Quebec family economy brought those families to Manchester and other New England textile mill cities in the first place. Poverty from soil depletion, increasing competition from western agriculture, and land scarcity from growing families had forced Quebec families to seek opportunity elsewhere by late nineteenth century. While the first immigrants may have come as individuals, they were rapidly followed, through a process of "chain migration," by brothers, sisters, parents, cousins, uncles and aunts, and neighbors.

If "chain migration" brought Franco-Americans to Manchester and elsewhere, the imperatives of family economies put them to work and kept them at work. For the household economy to function under a low wage structure, all family members—parents and children, male and female—needed to work and pool their incomes for family survival. Probably the most difficult period for family financial survival were those years between when a young mother quit work to bear children and when the oldest child entered the mill in late childhood. The best times were those years when the household economy consisted of the wages of a working father and mother and those of their adolescent children still living at home. During the difficult period, as the narrative of "a Franco-American grandmother" would suggest, the young mother or young children might be sent back to the Quebec farm for awhile.

"Chain employment" facilitated this full employment. Until the Amoskeag's establishment of an employment office on the eve of World War I, most Franco-Americans gained their first employment by having a relative intervene on their behalf with the supervisory personnel in the factory room where the relative already worked. If the relative was reliable, and there was a job opening, the new family member was hired. One would start in an unskilled job in a room where one of the various textile-manufacturing functions occurred, such as carding, spinning, or weaving. Most of the work in each of those rooms was machine-tending, done by semi-skilled or skilled workers. As long as the machines ran well, the relative had time to supervise or look out for the new arrival. By watching the machine-tenders or by receiving instruction from a machine-tending relative, the unskilled family member could learn more advanced skills and move into better jobs in the same room. According to his narrative, Philippe Lemay was not quite typical. He started as an unskilled roving boy in the card room, which converted bales of cotton or wool in rovings ready for spinning. Ordinarily he would have moved onto one of the various machines in the carding process. Instead, he went on to be an unskilled bobbin boy in a spinning room and then advanced, in the usual way, to a ring-spinner. Interestingly enough, he chose that over learning the more difficult and arduous mule-spinning. For most Franco-Americans, then, kinship provided young family members with employment entry and advancement; older family members covered for younger members when they did not feel well or do well; and in turn, all employed family members contributed their wages to the common household economy. To some extent, kinship provided the job security, the establishment of work rules, and paths to advancement one ordinarily would expect from trade unions.

Kinship's ability to affect the workplace broke down in the twentieth century, requiring Franco-American workers to resort to new techniques. The breakdown resulted from the Amoskeag's response to rising competition by new, more productive southern mills. Rather than investing in new machinery as productive as that in the South, the Amoskeag instituted "scientific management" principles to get more work out of the existing machines and people. Before World War I, the Amoskeag replaced the informal employment recruitment procedures with a central employment office. After the war, the company, like other New England textile companies, sought profitability through the "speed-up" and "stretch-out," requiring faster work tending more machines, and pay-cuts. Although Philippe Lemay's narrative paints a rosy picture of worker-overseer relations, Tamara Hareven's account of grievance proceedings, a right won by workers during the war, indicates that overseers had become "men with little tolerance for the workers, men who harbored grudges and played favorites." In short, by the early 1920s, the old mutuality between overseers and workers in job recruitment and workrules had broken down and company paternalism had turned toward company exploitation.

In this new situation, Amoskeag workers increasingly turned to trade unionism. When the Amoskeag and other New England textile companies cut pay and lengthened hours in 1922, Franco-Americans joined other Amoskeag workers in going out on strike. After nine months, the strike was broken. The company continued its decline, and worker demoralization grew apace. After another strike in 1933, the Amoskeag closed its doors forever in 1935.

The Franco-American workers interviewed by Tamara Hareven and her team recalled most vividly the Manchester of the Amoskeag's decline and demise. The life-history narratives which follow recall, instead, the Manchester of the Amoskeag's heyday, the world which was lost. The Philippe Lemay of the first narrative appears to be a pseudonym or, perhaps, a composite. To some extent it resembles the career of Théophile Biron, the first Franco-American overseer at the Amoskeag and the founding president of the Association Canado-Américaine. Henri Lemay was a Manchester jeweler.

FOR FURTHER READING

Steve Dunwell, *The Run of the Mill: A Pictorial Narrative of the Expansion, Dominion, Decline and Enduring Impact of the New England Textile Industry,* Boston: David R. Godine Publisher, 1978.

Tamara K. Hareven and Randolph Langenbach, *Amoskeag: Life and Work in an American Factory-City,* New York: Pantheon Books, 1978.

Tamara K. Hareven, *Family Time and Industrial Time: The Relationship Between the Family and Work in a New England Industrial Community,* Cambridge: Cambridge University Press, 1982.

Philippe Lemay

I was born in St. Ephrem d'Upton, P.Q., not far from St. Hyacinthe and Montreal, June 29, 1856. I was the fourth in a family of fourteen children, five of whom are still living. It took us four days and as many nights to go from our hometown, St. Ephrem d'Upton, to Lowell in 1864. Train engines weren't big and powerful in those days. Besides, they were wood-burners, and you couldn't put enough wood in the tender to make long trips. So trains didn't run far and never during the night. We started from St. Ephrem in the afternoon and went as far as Sherbrooke and slept there. The next day, we reached Island Pond, Vermont, and spent the night in that customs town. It was a very small place, too. The following morning, the old Grand Trunk took us to Portland, Maine, and again we passed the night there, because the train went no further. After another night's rest, on a different railroad, we were on our way to Boston where we had to find lodgings once more. At last, the fifth day, we landed in Lowell where we were to live for eight years.

Many things can happen on such long trips, and something did while we were coming to the States, *aux Etats,* as French Canadians say it even today. At Island Pond, my mother was taken sick and couldn't go on with us when we left for Portland on the third day of our journey. Father remained with her. We were told to continue towards Lowell and to mind our uncle and aunt who were making the trip with us from St. Ephrem. We promised to be good and followed our good aunt and uncle, but we worried on account of our parents. We weren't separated for long, though, for mother was a strong, healthy woman, of good Canadian stock. Father and mother arrived in Lowell only three days after we did, and what do you think they brought with them? A new little Lemay whom we all welcomed to our already rather large family.

When we landed at Lowell in 1864, there were very few French Canadians, only five families at one end of the city, fifteen at the other. Many more came after the Civil War was over. I was only eight years old, but that didn't stop me from going to work. My first job as a textile worker was in the Lawrence mill, No. 5, where I worked as a bagboy and doffer for about three years. Then I wanted to do outside work and one of my jobs was driving a one-horse wagon. In 1872, when I was sixteen, our family moved to Manchester. In 1875, father and mother returned to St. Ephrem.

Here, in the beginning, I started in a card room as roving and bobbin boy, but I wanted to be a spinner, not a mule-spinner. I had seen mule-spinning in Lowell and didn't like it at all; fly-spinning that makes cotton into thread, ready for the weave-room, that's what I wanted to do. But it wasn't until 1875, the year my folks went back to Canada for good, that I got my chance. How I landed in No. 1 spinning mill of the Amoskeag, where no French Canadian could be hired before, is a little story in itself.

Each spring and fall, it seems, the older immigrants had a touch of homesickness. Most of them still had farms in old Quebec. "I want to see if it is still where I left it," they'd smilingly tell the boss when they asked permission to be away for five or six weeks. So they went back to Canada twice a year. While there, they visited friends and relatives, that's sure, but their principal reason was a serious one, and they had to make many sacrifices in order to save up enough money to pay railroad fares and other necessary expenses.

At heart, Monsieur, they were still farmers like their ancestors had been, and they wanted to get something out of those farms, some of which had been in the family for many generations. In the spring, they attended to ploughing, harrowing and sowing; in the fall, to the harvesting of the crops. During the summer, some relative or neighbor kindly gave a look once in awhile to see that all was well.

While they were absent from the mills—others having to loaf on account of sickness or for some other reason—sparehands had their chance to work. That's how I got into spinning. The overseer was kept at home by sickness and the second hand hired me. When the boss came back, I was giving all my attention to my work and not losing a minute. We all did that. But the overseer didn't look pleased and he was mad when his assistant told him my name. He wanted to know why I had been hired when he didn't want any Frenchman working there in his mill. The second hand said he'd discharge me right away and I felt that my dream of becoming a fly-spinner was coming to an end quickly. I kept on working. The boss looked at me, seemed to think twice before he spoke and then said: "Don't do it now; wait until Smith comes back to work."

Smith did come back and I was out of a job, but not for long. The boss was sorry to let me go, that was plain. He took my address and said he'd let me know as soon as he needed me. He had changed his mind about hiring French Canadians after he had seen one of them at work. The very next day, at noon, he sent for me and after that I had a regular job in the Amoskeag. And that same boss hired many of my people, and that is the point I want to bring out in my story.

Later, I was transferred to No. 4 mill where there were, besides the overseer, three second hands in a department of 18,000 spindles. You can imagine how little work those assistant overseers had to do. They ought to have been running some of the frames to keep themselves busy. I went back to No. 1 with a job that paid me $1.30 a day, 20 cents more than I was getting at No. 4. I was roving-boy, oiled the shafts and pulleys and did other jobs.

The boss of No. 4 mill wanted me back and offered me $1.45 a day. I went, of course. One day, another overseer tried to get me, and when I spoke of leaving, Hamilton, boss of No. 4 wouldn't hear of it. To keep me, he offered me extra pay if I would do the work of a sickly operative who had to loaf at times, and more extra pay if I wanted to take the place of a third hand once in a while. I accepted, did my own work besides and, as long as the arrangement lasted, I got $2 a day and a little more. I was finally given a regular job as third hand, quite a promotion for a French Canadian at the time. In 1881, I was made second hand and, in 1901, overseer in No. 1 spinning mill. It included No. 2, where I had such a hard time getting a small job twenty-six years before.

It was a big event when I was appointed overseer of the 1 and 8 spinning mills. There was to be a vacancy very shortly. I knew about it and, being convinced that no one would say a good word for me, I decided to speak for myself. I wasn't bashful any more. So, one day, I asked the super if he wouldn't give me the chance. He was so surprised that he couldn't speak for a long time, or so it seemed to me. He was looking at me as if he had been struck by thunder and lightning. What! A Frenchman had the crust to think he could be an overseer! That was something unheard of, absolutely shocking. And the super was shocked, I'm telling you. When he recovered enough to speak, he told me he'd think it over, turned his back on me and walked off. He was certainly upset.

The next day, he came to me and, still with a doubting expression spread all over his face, said he'd try me for six months. But I didn't want six months, I answered back. I wasn't going to clog up that spinning department. Either I was the man for the job, I said, or I wasn't. If I was, it wouldn't take six months to find out. If I wasn't, I'd get out in a hurry. No six months for me. One month, that's all I wanted to show what I could do. The super seemed to be wondering again but answered it was all right with him just as I said. So I became the overseer of No. 1 spinning where I had made my shaky *début* in 1875.

That was another step ahead for the French Canadians, wasn't it? But this time, it was an awful scandal. The sad news didn't take long to spread. Americans and Irish were mad clean through. They looked at me and spoke to me only when they were strictly obliged to, but as far as friendship was concerned, there was no more, you bet. I, a Frenchman, had jumped over the heads of others who thought themselves the only ones entitled to the job of overseer; here was a sin that could not be forgiven, and what was the world coming to, anyway?

My disappointed former friends had another shock of the same kind two years later when Théophile Marchand—we called him Tofil—was named overseer of weaving, and he was included with me in their hate. Tofil, who had been a first class weaver, was then a first class loomfixer, a big job in those days. His promotion, like mine, became the talk of "Milltown" and was a terrible scandal.

Later, those who were afraid of us got used to these things and took them in a better spirit, for several other French Canadian textile workers got well deserved promotions. Théophile Marchand, better known as John, was one of my own second hands, and I recommended him. He was a boss just three days, then he came back to his old job with me, after telling the superintendent that he'd be happier and healthier that way. "An overseer's job has too many worries," he said. "The first thing you know, I'd be loafing because I was sick, and I can't afford to do that, because I have quite a family to support." And so, my friend Tofil had the distinction of being the first French Canadian, perhaps the first one of my nationality group, to refuse an overseer's job.

Others who didn't worry were a Mr. Lalime who was made a superintendent of weaving; Frank Houde who came with me to the Coolidge mill as a second hand and went later to No. 1 spinning mill as an overseer; Wilfred Lemay, one of my sons, who was second hand for the one who took my place as boss of old No. 1 when I was transferred to the Coolidge in May, 1910. There then was Domicile Nolet, superintendent of carding at the Stark Mills, and a M. Blais, overseer of spinning for the same company, when Amoskeag bought Stark in 1922. They stayed as bosses for the Amoskeag until it shut down for good. M. Nolet became overseer for the Pacific Mills who opened a plant here a few years ago in a part of old Amoskeag. Pacific moved to Dover this year; Domicile followed and is still there.

An overseer had a good chance to get even with those who hate him and have been mean to him and his people, but such a thought didn't come to my mind. As soon as I had been appointed, the super came over and said to me: "Lemay, now is the time to get rid of your second hand. He never liked you and he's no good anyway. You are now able to discharge him and pay him back what he did to you." "I'm giving this man a chance to make good with me if he wants to. Besides, he's just as good as I am. I won't punish him or anybody else that way because I have been treated meanly. Don't expect me to get rid of John until I have good reason to, and that goes for all those who work under me." So I kept my first second hand. I recommended him to take my place in No. 1 when I was transferred to the New Coolidge mill. Again the super couldn't understand me. "But can he do the job?" he asked. "Sure," I answered, "even better than I can." "There you are again," replied the big boss. "Whether it's to keep a second hand I don't want or to get him the job of overseer, you insist he's a better man than you, and the man isn't a French Canadian either." "He doesn't have to be one of my people, Mr. Super. If he's all right, I say so, and that's justice. Go ahead and try him out and find out what a fine man he is." The super did, the man made good and I had my revenge twice against John, a Christian's revenge. I got no credit for what I had done but wasn't disappointed. My own good luck has brought me the congratulations and good wishes of only one American official, the superintendent of the machine shops. The others kept their grudge until the time to congratulate has passed and then made the best of a thing that couldn't be avoided.

Ask any French Canadian textile worker and he will tell you how well he got along with his overseer. We got along well because we never killed time, gave our attention to our jobs and turned out work that the company could sell. That is why we got the reputation of being skillful operatives who could be trusted to remain on the jobs even if the bosses weren't always around to watch them. It is for that same reason the local textile corporations sent agents to Canada and to American textile centers to bring more of those French Canadians.

Our American overseers were always fair and just to us and it is fair and just to admit it. They were fine men and knew their business. They never bothered those who did their duty. We can certainly be thankful to them for their decent treatment of us. Stanislas Gagnon tells this story to prove it.

"My second hand," says Gagnon, "was an Irish-American who took away some work from a Irish operative. It was extra work for me without any extra pay. At first, being a little timid, I told the second boss I'd do the work, but the more I thought it over afterward, the more convinced I was the second hand was favoring his countryman at my own expense, and I refused to be anybody's goat. I went to my overseer and told him all about it. He thought I was right and told me so. He then went to the Irish assistant boss and asked him if what I had said was true. The second hand admitted it was and went on to say that I lost a lot of time talking with women operatives and killed time otherwise. Speaking louder, he continued: "He has plenty of time to do this extra work I gave him and he's going to do it or somebody's going to get out." To which the boss answered: "Yes, somebody's going to get out and it won't be Gagnon. I'm keeping him, so you'd better change your mind pretty soon about that extra work you gave him, because he isn't going to do it. Think it over if you care anything for your job." The second hand changed his mind in a hurry and the Irish operative got his work back again.

The overseer trusted Gagnon, that is why he stood by him. The company itself had much confidence in us and gave us big and important tasks to do. Not the least of these was the job of getting up the machinery and putting in operation the spinning department in the new Coolidge Mill in 1910. We started in May. In December, the executives were told the job had been completed. They couldn't believe that it had taken only seven months, and only a personal investigation could convince them. If all those who worked with me hadn't given their full cooperation, it couldn't have been done, so the greater part of the credit belongs to them. We had set up in record time what was said to be the largest single spinning department in the world, 105,000 spindles and 450 hands on one floor, and there were also the picker-room men in the basement. Many French Canadians worked for me and my first assistant was Théophile Marchand.

Because of working I had no schooling at all when I was a boy, and none until I had been made a second hand, and that was in 1881. I had three terms at evening school, each term beginning in October and ending sometime in March. Afterward, I took one term in a business college, again attending evening classes, of course. When I started to go to school, I already could speak English pretty well, and that was a great help to me.

When I was a young boy in Lowell, my father wanted me to attend day school, but I didn't care much for reading, writing, spelling and arithmetic. Father left home early in the morning to go to work in the sawmill, as he had to walk about a mile and a half, coming back only for supper. As soon as he was gone, I went in my turn, but not to school; I went to the mills. At night, I got a good spanking, this happening every day, but I couldn't change my ways. I wanted to work, that's all, to do something for my parents who needed all the help they could get, with the family they had to feed and take care of. Father had to let me have my way, but he didn't like to and showed it more than once.

In general, French Canadian children living here could have had some schooling in the grammar school grades if their parents had been able to get along without the earnings of these boys and girls, but most of them couldn't afford that. The only ones who had a chance to get an education were the youngest of the children, because older brothers and sisters were in the mills, helping their parents at the time.

There were difficult moments in the lives of these young mill workers. If they happened to be loafing, they were generally out on the streets. Sometimes, a truant officer would come along and ask questions. Why weren't the boys in school? How old were they? Where did they live? They were in hot water all the time this third degree business lasted. They had to think up some reasonable answers in not too much time in order to satisfy the officer and keep their jobs in the mills. If they had been forced to go to school, the loss of their small earnings, added together, would have made quite a difference in the family budget.

The 1922 strike lasted nearly ten months and was the worst thing that ever happened. It was bad for the city, its merchants, tenement owners, business in general. It destroyed Amoskeag's trade and the Company, never recovering from the blow, kept going down until it had to close its doors. My sympathy, however, goes first to all the workers for they are the ones who suffered the most. They lost all their savings, went deep in debt and lived on canned beans while the hope of winning the fight was kept dangling before their eyes. They were told almost every day by the strike leaders to be patient and tighten up their belts because victory was in sight. But there was no victory, only defeat for all concerned.

As an overseer, I couldn't join their ranks in the labor union nor help them in any way, but neither could I be against them. As a boy, a young man and a middle-aged man with a family, I had worked long hours for anything but high wages. I knew what it meant to be poor, what sacrifices must be made if you want to lay something aside for a rainy day. The workers wanted more pay; I would have given them a living wage if it had been in my power to do so, every worker having a right to that. They wanted shorter hours; I would have given them a reasonable work week if I had anything to say about it. Even as a second hand and an overseer, I never forgot my humble beginnings and always considered myself a textile worker. Those strikers were textile workers too, and I was sorry for them. Yes, that strike of 1922 was really a terrible thing.

Why did our people leave Canada and come to the States? Because they had to make sure of a living for their family and themselves for a number of years, and because they greatly needed money. The wages paid by textile mills was the attraction.

Here and wherever else they went, they didn't like to become citizens and feared it for more than one reason. They couldn't speak English, and that, let me tell you, was a big handicap. They were afraid of war and might be drafted. Most of them were still tax-payers in the Province of Quebec and the different places from which they came, and they felt that they couldn't pay taxes here too. Most of them hadn't come here to stay. What they wanted most was to go back to their Canadian farms with the money earned in the textile mills. So they kept putting off taking out naturalization papers.

But we already had able leaders, among them Ferdinand Gagnon, editor of *La Voix du Peuple*, and they preached Americanization to all those who intended to stay in this country. They pointed it out as a duty to ourselves as well as to the country. They told us that naturalization was something that gave to a foreigner all the rights belonging to the citizen of the country to which the foreigner swears allegiance. Our people began to realize that their ideas against being naturalized were wrong. They saw privileges as well as the duties, and so, as early as 1871, we had fifty voters in Manchester, fifty men who, supporting Father Chevalier, were able to obtain from the city authorities without cost to the French-speaking Catholics, a French language school: building, heating, lights, books and lay teachers. This success was encouraging. Naturalization increased, and that, if you take account of the many births, tells you why so many of us are voters and tax-payers today, why so many of our folks settled here for all time.

The majority of French Canadian immigrants came to Manchester at their own expense. In fact, all of them did, so far as I know, and they didn't have to be coaxed, either. It is true that some companies, seeing in the *type québécois* an honest, able workman, asking little for himself and rather unwilling to let himself be fooled by strike agitators, brought here a certain number through recruiting agents sent to Canada for the purpose. The companies built homes to house these new hands. However, if their fares and other expenses were paid by the textile corporations, it was never mentioned and I don't believe it was done.

Our people didn't come to the States with money they had saved up, though, since they emigrated because they were really obliged to go where they could earn their daily bread and butter. To raise enough money to buy railroad tickets for the family and pay for food, rooms and other expenses en route, they had to *faire encan,* sell all their household goods at auction. That money was practically all gone when they arrived here, and all they possessed was the clothes they had on their backs, you might say. Parents and children alike were dressed in homespun and homemade clothes and they were recognized as coming from Quebec province the very moment they left the train. Most of them, you see, were from small towns and farming districts, very few coming from large cities like Montreal and Quebec. As they were poor, all those who were old enough went to work without waiting to take a much needed rest.

They boarded at first with relatives, if they were lucky enough to have any here, or with some French Canadian family until they could rent a tenement for themselves, mostly in corporation houses, and buy the furniture that was strictly needed.

Money was very precious to us in those days and we spent it carefully, getting along with only the things we couldn't do without, but we were able to make a living and save something besides. You understand that food, clothing, lodging, fuel, everything was much cheaper then than now. For lighting, we used kerosene lamps and the streets were lighted the same way. It was some time later that we had gas.

Our kitchen had to serve also as dining room and living room. There was no such thing as a parlor and no place for one, because all the other rooms, including the front one, were bedrooms and there weren't too many, you can bet on that. We had no draperies or sash curtains in the windows, just paper shades without roller springs such as we saw later. A narrow strip of wood, of the same width, was sold with this paper shade and we nailed it across the top to the window frame. In the morning, the shade was rolled up by hand and held up by a string fastened to a nail. The floors, not always of hard wood, were bare and had to be scrubbed on hands and knees with lye or some other strong stuff, once a week at least, on Saturdays. The only floor coverings we knew were round braided carpets and *catalognes*, seven or eight feet long and three wide, homemade with rags carefully put away for that purpose.

Once a week, sometimes twice, our women folks broke their backs over the washboard and wrung the family washing by hand, washing machines and wringers being unknown at the time. There was no hot water in large, convenient tanks, only what you heated on the kitchen stove in the washboiler, pans and pots, or if you came to afford it, a teakettle. This hot water served for cooking, washing the dishes, clothes and floors and to take the weekly bath in the wash tub.

But we had big appetites and ate well and slept well, going to bed and getting up early every day in the week, except Sunday. Sunday nights, we had our *veillées du bon vieux temps*, as we had them in Canada. The younger folks enjoyed birthday parties, but early French Canadian textile workers, even in the 'seventies, never thought of celebrating their golden or silver wedding anniversaries. In 1871, our first parish was established and our new church, St. Augustin's, was opened in 1873. A few years later, we had two parishes, so we really could practice our religion as easily as we did in old Quebec. We said our morning prayer separately, but after supper, before the dishes were washed, we recited the beads and evening prayer *en famille*, father or mother alternating with the children and the boarders.

After a while, the children became young men and women. They had been earning money for a few years and, being prouder, thought of changing from homespuns, worn every Sunday, to more fashionable store clothes. We saved pennies until they became dollars and when there was enough, we dressed up, you bet, paying in full for what we bought, not a little down and so much a week, as so many do today with the creation and the spread of the installment plan.

Where did we meet the girls we married? Why right here in Manchester. No, we weren't in love before we left Canada. We were too young to think of such things when we came to the States. Very few had known in childhood the girls they were going to marry; so many of us, you see, came from different parishes and villages.

The young lady who became my wife in 1878 was Miss Selima Laliberté. She lived in a private home, that of her friend, Miss Laurence, who kept house with her two brothers and worked in the mills besides. Now Damase and Georges Laurence, Moise Verette, and Joseph Baril and myself were intimate friends. Joe Baril's mother wasn't in good health and I had only one small room, so we spent our evenings together with the Laurences or at the home or Moise Verette. While visiting Georges and Damase, I became acquainted with Miss Laliberté. She was a fine, attractive girl and interested me. Soon I was going to the Laurence home mostly to see Selima, then for herself alone. We had fallen in love, we became engaged and were married by Father Chevalier in St. Augustin's church.

Joe Pellerin found his wife in Canada; she was a stranger to him. He went to Yamachiche in the late summer of 1891 while on vacation after an illness. He was coaxed to take a job in a general store at Maskinongé, only a few miles away. He got the job and stayed thirteen months. His pay was five dollars a month with room and board, but it was a lucky day for him, he says, when he went to Maskinongé, for it was there he met the girl he was to make his wife. He came back here in the spring of 1892, leaving his heart in the little Canadian village, and went to work for Adam Graf. In the fall of 1892, having decided not to wait any longer, he took the train for Maskinongé, married the girl he loved and brought her to Manchester where they have lived happily ever since.

We had family reunions, mostly on Sunday, to amuse ourselves. They were real *veillées canadiennes* and we certainly enjoyed ourselves. We sang without piano accompaniment songs of Old Quebec, danced square and round dances and jigs, played games like *L'assiette tournante* (Spin the Platter) for forfeits, and played cards for the fun of it, mostly euchre, a game we learned here.

Sometimes, one sang alone; at other times, we sang in chorus. There were also *chansons à répondre*, a solo with certain lines repeated in chorus by *la compagnie*, the gathering. Everybody who was asked to sing cleared his throat—that was the usual ceremony—saying he or she had a cold, and called on the others to help him: *Vous allez m'aider hein?*

What did we sing? Well, Monsieur, we sang *Vive la Canadienne* and other popular songs of the Canadian folklore; sentimental songs, and one of them—I don't remember all the words because I didn't sing much myself—began like this:

> C'est aujourd'hui le jour de mes noces,
> C'est aujourd'hui le plus beau de mes jours.

> Ah! oui, cher amant que j'aime.
> Je suis à toi aujourd'hui pour toujours.

I couldn't translate that in verse, but here is what it means: This is the day of my wedding, the happiest day of my life; beloved, I am yours forever.

Some were very good at singing comic songs, like *Zozo* in which the words are so misplaced that sense becomes nonsense, the kind that makes you laugh. I believe I remember the first verse. Here it is, and it's crazy.

> Je suis Zozo, par mes actions comiques,
> J'ai fait parler de moi pendant-z-onze ans.
> Je suis le fils de mon seul père unique
> Et pour le sur aussi bien de Mouman
> Un jour, la nuit, ce pauvre Valère
> Tomba malade, mon père me dit: Zozo,
> Va chercher du bouillon pour ta mère
> Qu'est bien malade là-bas dans un petit pot,
> Va chercher du bouillon pour ta mère,
> Qu'est bien malade là-bas dans un petit pot.

This part of another verse is even worse:

> Mais v'là t'y pas que ma maladresse
> Je chavirai les assiettes et les plats;
> Je fis une tache sur ma veste de graisse
> Et les culottes de ma jambe de drap. . . .

In the first, Zozo, the son of his only father, is told to fetch some broth for his mother who is sick over there in a little pitcher. In what there is of the second, Zozo knocks down the dishes and spills broth over his fat vest and the trousers of his woolen cloth leg.

Another song, this one a *chanson à répondre*, was a sort of a catechism and mentioned one God, two Testaments, etc. up to the Ten Commandments. As he went along, the singer, as we do in *Alouette*, repeated backwards what he had sung and finished as he had begun, with the words: *Il n'y a qu'un seul Dieu, Il n'y a qu'un seul Dieu*, which the others repeated after him in chorus.

For our round and square dances as well as jigs, the music was furnished by a fiddler who always played the same tune as long as you wanted him to—he knew no other—and by a fellow who played the accordian, but they never played together because their tunes were different. We didn't care about that and we danced and had great fun. In St. Ephrem, even these home dances weren't allowed because our people believed that the devil himself was present as a *cavalier* wherever people danced. Stories of tragic happenings were told and made you shiver. Here, we never went to public dance halls but weren't afraid of the devil being in our homes if we conducted ourselves as decent people should.

In 1874, Father Chevalier of St. Augustin's parish, wishing to encourage the study of music among his parishioners and to give more prestige to the French Canadians of Manchester, called a group of young men to his home and proposed that they should start a band. The idea was quickly accepted and in a short time and after much work, we had the *Fanfare Canadienne de Manchester* and it became an institution. It paraded many times in our city and gave concerts which were well attended. It was engaged by fraternal groups and travelled as far as Quebec. There were twenty-seven members in the *Fanfare*, called the French Military Band by the English newspapers. It was reorganized in 1882 as the City Band which ceased to exist only a few years ago. Father Chevalier's band was composed of textile workers and I played the slide trombone.

The days of petty persecution, beatings, rock-throwing, swill-slinging and tragedy from Irish people are not nice to remember. They were afraid that we had come here to take their jobs away from them in the mills and they tried hard to send us back to Canada by making life impossible for us in America. They wanted us to speak the English among ourselves when we only knew French, and it made them mad because we didn't. They had forgotten—or didn't know—that French Canadians had taken into their homes many orphaned children of Irish immigrants to Canada and brought them up as their own. Yes, Irish Americans should have been our best friends over here, not out worst enemies.

It was bad enough here in 1872 and later, but it was worse in Lowell about 1864. It was impossible to get drinking water from public pumps in the daytime. Irish boys threw dirt in our pails, so we had to go at night, in the darkness and by roundabout ways.

Sundays, we went to mass at the Irish church. There was no other. Irish lads sat behind us and, with needles or pins stuck in the end of their books, they'd dig into us. We jumped and yelled, and other people in the church were disturbed. We had our ears boxed by the man in charge of children. When we couldn't stand it any longer, we stopped going to church. The priest visited our homes to inquire about our absence. We told him why we stayed at home, the guilty boys got a licking and then we could attend Sunday services in peace.

My father worked in a sawmill located almost in the center of the city. For a time, the men were obliged to work at night and the owners had to build a shack where the workers could eat their lunch without fear of being injured or killed by rocks thrown at them. The job was lit up by flaming rosin placed in large iron pans, but all around the place it was very dark. So, it was easy to hide and throw rocks or bricks and you'd never know where they came from.

Irishmen were fond of clay pipes, "T.D.s," they were called, but they must have thought nobody else had the right to use the same kind. When they met a French Canadian smoking a clay pipe, they'd break it off between his teeth. If he'd smoke a briar pipe, they'd push it down his throat. Not liking this sort of sport, our fathers and big brothers smoked nothing but short "T.D.s" that couldn't be shortened any more nor pushed in.

In Manchester, it was in those parts of the city where only Irish people lived, especially what was called *l'Irlande*, all around Park Common which was called *la commune d'Irlande*, that we found plenty of trouble. Our family was then living in the "Squog" section of West Manchester, and the shortest way to St. Augustin's church, the only French church at that time, was through the *commune d'Irlande*. Well, sir, we couldn't pass there without having our Sunday clothes ruined by filthy swill thrown at us from yards and alleys. Rocks flew also, and many of us youngsters received painful beatings from young Irish Americans who were nearly always armed with sticks. The only way for us to save our clothes and our skins was to go to the church by making a long detour and approaching St. Augustin's from the east instead of from the west as we would have naturally done if there had been no enemies on the way.

No, we didn't fight back, because we were afraid of having trouble with the law. Being strangers, we didn't know how it would turn out for us. The first Greeks who came to Manchester weren't so timid. Welcomed as we had been by the Irish, they thought they hadn't come from far-off Greece to be chased away without some resistance. They paid back with interest everything they received from the residents of the district. Often they were arrested but just as soon acquitted after they had proved that they had acted in self-defense. The Irish hated Chief of Police Healy for that, though he was an Irishman himself, but he was a just man and a fine chief who made Manchester the orderly city it is. Anyway, the Greeks did so well that the *commune d'Irlande* is now called the *commune des Grecs* where people may pass without being insulted or beaten up.

Some years later, French Canadian grown-ups were treated more decently. There were too many of us then and we weren't so bashful about defending ourselves. Irish boys alone remained mischievous. Armed with sticks and stones, they often chased French Canadian boys through streets and back yards, even into homes where the attacking "army" didn't always dare to follow.

But the worst blow struck at us was the killing of Jean-Baptiste Blanchette, a member of the French Band of which he was then the leader and a fine fellow if there ever was one.

On the night of September 30, 1880, Blanchette and four friends who also belonged to the band, were talking quietly about the *Fanfare* and its leadership, in French, of course, on Amherst St., near the corner of Vine. It was a little after 11 o'clock. Three Irish young men—no need of mentioning their names—came out of another beer parlor located nearby, on the same street. They, like many others, hated to hear French spoken and called on the five "frogs" to "talk United States." They rushed the French Canadians as they passed them. The three attackers were drunk. Blanchette pushed them away. One of the three came back at Jean-Baptiste who met him once more, and the assailant, either struck or pushed, fell on the sidewalk. A large, round beer bottle, containing a small quantity of hard liquor, was broken in the fall. The man was furious. He got back on his feet, seized the upper part of the broken bottle and holding it by the neck, he threw it and it struck Blanchette on the left side of the throat. Blanchette had run into the street and there he fell. The jagged edge of the broken bottle had made a wound one inch deep and two inches long and cut the jugular vein. Blanchette was soon bathing in his blood which was coming out so fast nobody could stop the flow.

Quickly, Blanchette's friends picked him up and carried him to his room over the saloon. They laid him down on the floor where another pool of blood was soon formed. There was now a wide, sticky red trail leading from the street, onto the sidewalk and the stairs and into the room. A piece of glass, the pointed end sticking out, was still in the wound. It was removed and one of Blanchette's companions held his hand over the gaping hole, trying to stop the constant flow of blood. He died twenty minutes after being hit, having lost all his blood.

The news spread like wild fire around the usually quiet city. The next morning, at 7 o'clock, hundreds of French Canadians stood near the corner of Vine and Amherst Streets. The bloody spot was still there and staring at it, they said: "This is where three Irishmen killed Jean Blanchette last night." The crowd was excited and you could hear a low grumbling, but there was no other demonstration. They held themselves as they had done whenever thay had been made to suffer. Only this was worse and could hardly be believed. A man had been killed by a "frog" hater. Those hundreds of men could have cried as if Blanchette had been the near relative of all of them while they kept looking at that awful red spot which nobody had thought of cleaning up.

The Irish lads were arrested and locked up in cells at the police station. Two were charged with being drunk and fined, being held afterward as witnesses. The bottle thrower who admitted throwing the top half of the beer bottle but insisted he didn't know where it landed, was accused of murder. At the

January term of Superior Court, he was sentenced to five years in prison. He served his sentence and died a few months after coming out. He was only 18 years old at the time of the tragedy, his father and mother were dead and he lived here with an uncle. He had worked in the mills but had been idle for some time.

Jean-Baptiste Blanchette was 23 years of age and had come to Manchester thirteen years before. He had worked for the Amoskeag in a weave room in the Langdon mill. Later, though still a young man, he had saved up enough money to run two small lager beer parlors where French Canadians liked to gather and talk of the things that interested them. They had no social clubs at the time.

Blanchette wasn't married. He roomed with the family of Alexandre Boucher and boarded at 22 Concord St. His body was laid out at the home of his good friend, M. Harrington, 51 Pearl St. The funeral took place at St. Augustin's church on Sunday morning, October 2nd, at 9 o'clock. As early as 7 o'clock, there was a large crowd of French Canadians in front of the Harrington home. At half past eight the long funeral procession started its march to the church.

In front was the *Fanfare Canadienne*. Then came the *Société St. Jean-Baptiste*, 104 members wearing their insignia and carrying their banners. Blanchette had been voted in as a member but had not yet signed the society's constitution and by-laws, so he wasn't an active member, but the *Société* turned out just the same. From 200 to 300 young men, all intimate friends of Blanchette, marched in ranks behind the hearse. There was also the French Republican Club of which John was a member. Then followed carriages in which were Blanchette's relatives. His father lived somewhere in New Hampshire but no one knew his address. Following the carriages in the procession were about 1,000 persons of all ages. Crowds lined the streets on the way to the church and all seemed to sympathize with the relatives who escorted the body. In a few minutes, the church was filled. Father Chevalier officiated at the high mass for the dead and gave absolution. On the casket we could see the uniform our friend wore and the cornet he played in the band, with a crown of natural flowers made by Miss Emelie Harrington.

After the church services the procession was formed just as it had been before and marched to St. Augustin's cemetery, in the southern end of the city, where the body was buried.

Only a few hours before Blanchette met his death, I had visited him at his room. I was terribly shocked when I heard what had happened. He was a very dear friend of mine, always cheerful, quiet, minding his own business, kind to everybody. I asked myself how anyone could have struck him down in this awful manner just because he was talking to fellow-countrymen in the language that was most natural to him, his mother tongue. I can't understand now, after almost sixty years.

That tragic episode of 1880 brought much grief to the French Canadian colony, and compared to it, the mean things that had been done to us seemed very small indeed. Feelings ran high among us, but not one of us thought of avenging our murdered friend. As always we suffered in silence with the hope that some day our right to live peacefully in America would be recognized. We had so much confidence in God and in this adopted country of ours. Well, the day did come. Now the surviving French Canadian textile workers of long ago, their children, grandchildren, and great-grandchildren have won the respect and esteem of their fellow-citizens. Yes, we surely have found our place in the sun of American liberty. Franco-Americans are prominent in all lines of business and many are quite successful in politics. Since 1918, Manchester has had four mayors and they were all Franco-Americans. We have distinguished doctors, lawyers, educators, judges, artists, architects, bankers and clergymen, one of these having been the third bishop of Manchester for 25 years.

Today, we live in other times and fit ourselves to new conditions. The workweek has been considerably shortened and there is talk of making it even shorter. Machinery has been perfected, everything is modern. Between yesterday and today, what a difference! During my fifty-three years in the local mills, I have seen a seventy-five percent improvement. New looms in which the machine stopped if a thread broke were introduced about 1885 and saved much time and cloth. Ring-spinning succeeded fly-spinning with fine results for everybody. In 1872, the mills made fancy shirting, fleeced and plain cotton cloth, as well as blue and brown drilling for frocks and overalls; then came gingham and ticking and finally woolens, worsteds, every kind of textile product.

People work as hard now as they did years ago, but life is better, easier, more satisfactory for the mill worker of the present time and we old timers are glad that it is so. We are glad that we have brought it about to a certain extent. We are proud and insisted on working for our living, instead of depending on charity. We wanted to better our condition, own our home, set aside something against a rainy day, give our children a better education than we had ourselves. So we did our work honestly and well in order to keep our jobs and get better ones. Out of our wages we built churches, then schools, while supporting public schools and the government of our country, state and city. Our children, better educated, are already in higher positions or prepared to fill them with honor. Some of us have retired to the homes we worked so hard to buy, while others have bought farms and gone back to the occupation which was that of their fathers and ancestors in the country where we were born.

When we came here in 1872, we lived in "Squog," on the west side of the river. After I was married, I occupied the same tenement for 44½ years in an Amoskeag corporation house, on the north side of Stark St., between Elm and Canal Sts. For the last ten years, we have lived in this cottage I own on Candia Rd., near Lake Massabesic. I have with me my granddaughter, the housekeeper, and her son, 17 years old and a freshman at St. Anselm's College.

I have always loved to travel, especially since I have been out of the mills. I have a son living in Florida and I have spent seven or eight winters with him. I drove my car both ways every time. This year, again by automobile, I went to Canada three times. No, I haven't forgotten my birthplace where father, mother and others of my family are buried.

I use glasses to read, but when it comes to see from a distance my eyes are just as good as they were fifty years ago. Do I eat well? *Mon cher ami,* I can eat baked beans for supper and not feel the worse for it. I do quite a bit of work around the house. From spring until fall I take care of my garden. My granddaughter thinks I work too much and often scolds me in a nice way. You hear her scold even now, but look at her smile. When I'm not working, I read and that brings me to a little nap in my rocking-chair. When you are going on 83, you too will like your *petit somme* in the afternoon. I am still considered the head of the family, loved and respected. With all that, who wouldn't be happy in his old days? As you see, we are able to speak English without a trace of accent, and that is natural. I have been in this country so long and the children were all born here.

After working for over sixty years, stomach ulcers began to bother me. I thought I wouldn't be able to go on any longer and spoke of leaving the mills, but they didn't want to let me go. The company in May and June, 1924 gave me a vacation with pay and told me that would put me on my feet. I did come back in July but things went from bad to worse with my stomach. In December I was forced to retire and the Amoskeag, giving me a month's extra pay, had to let me quit my job as overseer of the Coolidge spinning mill. I went to the hospital where I spent quite a while and recovered my health.

I like the people who were with me in the mills and I sympathized with them. I helped them as anybody else would have done in my place. Did I, when I was boss, hide some who weren't quite sixteen when inspectors visited the mills? I wouldn't have mentioned that if you hadn't put the question, but there is some truth in it, though I wonder who could have told you. You see, I started working in the Lowell mills when I was only eight years old and I could understand. If boys and girls were big and strong enough to work, even if they were a little under the legal age, I gave them a chance to keep their jobs. Their parents were poor and needed every cent they could get. So I'd tell these younger workers to keep out of sight until the inspector had gone away. There was no harm to anybody in that and it did a lot of good. And besides, the law wasn't so strict in those days. Looking back over the years, when I think of those who worked with me and for me, I feel in my heart that I miss a lot of friends and I'd be lonesome at times if I didn't have something to keep me busy around here.

To what do we owe our success? I believe we owe it to the self-sacrificing French Canadian immigrants from Old Quebec, to the courage that made them refuse to accept defeat and quit when that would have seemed the natural thing to do, to the cheerfulness that carried us through our trials and tribulation and helps us old-timers to wait happily for the final bell calling us home to rest after our long, hard life in the textile mills. And perhaps the bloody death of Jean-Baptiste Blanchette, a martyr in the true sense of the word, had its share in bringing about the conditions we are enjoying today.

A Franco-American Grandmother

I have lived here a little more than fifty years. Fifty years, it is a long time, and yet, I remember what happened then as if it was yesterday. A few days before we began the trip to the States, I went to the village with my father. He had to see about tickets, the transportation of the few things we were going to take with us, the purchase of new clothes for us children, the payment of bills, etc.

We went to the general store, where we could find everything we needed. I'll never forget this hour. My father told Mr. B., the merchant, that he had decided to leave his farm and go to the United States to make money by working in the cotton mills with his two oldest daughters and also the other children, as soon as they would be old enough. Mr. B. seemed greatly distressed.

"Oh! no, no, don't do that, Joe," he said.

"But, Mr. B., I am a poor man. I have not enough land to make a success of agriculture. I can't buy enough cows. In fact, I cannot *venir à bout de mes affaires* if I stay here. My brother, who has gone to the States, writes us that he is making money. He has four children working in the mills."

"Yes, yes, working in the mills, *sapriste!*" interrupted Mr. B. "But, my good Joseph, think of what you will give, not only of what you will receive! You are going to make your children into slaves, spending their days behind thick, dirty walls, bound to some looms in the terrific and incessant noise. From six o'clock in the morning until six o'clock at night, they will be driven by some blind power, and then, they will fall into their beds in some crowded rooms, in order to gather enough strength to begin over again the next day.

"I know! I have seen these mills when I went for a business trip to Boston last year. I thought they were something inhuman, almost infernal. You and yours do not belong there, Joe. We are a rural race; our land is extraordinarily fertile and should be made to produce enough for all. If the Americans want to enlarge their manufacturing industry, very well, but our people should not be ensnared by them.

"Nothing hurts me more, nothing makes me sadder or more utterly discouraged for our future, than to see a Canadian—a man whose ancestors have opened this soil, have tilled it, have lived on it and now sleep under it—admit that he is willing to see his children spend their lives for the profit of these capitalists who draw hard gold from sweat and blood.

"You tell me that you are poor, Joe. No, you are not poor. A man is not poor who has all the substantial food he can eat, and all the wood he can burn. That is not poverty. When you open the door of your little house every morning you put your foot onto your own land. Ever think of that, Joe?

"Oh! you work hard, I know; your wife works hard too; but do you imagine that you won't work just as hard down there? Here you have space, air, and all the essentials of life, a little more perhaps. Your children are not dressed like city folks, but they are kept warm in the winter; they can laugh at our famous north wind when they are wrapped up to their necks in *bonne étoffe du pays* and above all, they grow up with the sense of a simple but very real dignity. They come from honest, decent stock and everybody knows it around here. The little luxuries that they might get out of their earnings will take away from them this so important feeling. They will be driven like cattle; they will be 'foreigners,' they will be 'immigrants.' As a rule, an immigrant is a poor devil who leaves his country because he is sure to suffer from hunger and cold if he stays."

All the time he was speaking, Mr. B. was standing in front of my father, who was listening to the low but firm voice, absolutely unable to give an answer to this vehement surge of words.

"You Canadian farmers are not proud enough of your profession. This goodly pride should be taught in school," mused Mr. B. after a moment of silence.

He sighed deeply, then made a step forward and offered his hand to my father.

"Well, goodbye and good luck to you, Joe, and to you, Miss Marie-Anne," said he with a smile in his fine, dark brown eyes. "Come back soon and marry an *habitant*."

Really, this scene has stayed in my mind as one of the most vital of all my life. Who knows? Perhaps it is from that moment that the idea germinated in me that it is of the greatest importance for a human being to adapt himself so as to be an integral part of the country where he lives his days.

Well, we came here and we worked in the mills. I began at eighteen, my sister at sixteen, then my two brothers when they were fifteen and thirteen, and last, my younger sister at fifteen. It was then the usual rule and nobody said anything against it. I realize now that it was not right, for while my sister and I were tall, had good strong bones, the three younger ones developed into puny-looking sickly adults. They are all dead now. I, the oldest, will be the last one to go.

Every summer when the mills were so hot that it was almost impossible to breathe inside them (many girls fainted every day), our parents sent my sisters and me for a visit with our uncles and aunts in Canada. I was interested in everything on the farm: chickens, ducks, calves, cute little pigs were a source of deep enjoyment for me. Oh! the thick, yellow cream, the small, sweet strawberries of the fields, the raspberries, blueberries we had there!

I used to tease and bother my aunts to teach me how to *travailler au métier* (carpet weaving on a handloom). I brought down a spinning wheel from the attic and learned how to spin. I knitted stockings, and I wove flannel and linen; of course, lace-making with a crochet or needles didn't keep any secret for me.

I am talking about 45 years ago. At the time there were no moving pictures, no theatres, except once in a while. In fact, amusements were great events. Every year, there was a bazaar in the parish; that was *our social event* in the whole twelve months! That was all the out-of-house diversion we had! Even the courting was done in the home under the jealous eye of the girl's mother.

When I was twenty-two, I was married. I had not much liked to work in the mill, but I had not let myself dislike it either. Girls were meek and submissive then; they did not have much to say about the arrangement of their lives. I was glad to start doing the real and only—so I have always believed—job for a woman: to be wife and mother.

I had learned very little English. But I had always liked books, and had been quite *appliquée* in my schoolwork at the convent in Canada. My young cousin was going to school here and, curiosity guiding me I think, I learned to read in English from her. But I never could find time or I was too tired to read anything. In one word, I lived the life of a *légume* for almost five years.

The first year of my married life was like a beautiful and serene recess after a hard day's work. I learned to cook and to sew a fine seam. I knitted and crocheted to my heart's content. As I was not as well as I should have been, my good husband made what he called a "big sacrifice" and sent me to Canada for a rest. But I did not rest very much, for during that month I wove some fifty yards of colorful *catalogne* which was cut to fit the length of the room, then sewed together (just like the old-fashioned carpeting). It covered entirely and very nicely the floor of what we were pleased to call *le salon*. I was proud of myself.

When I came back to Manchester (I suppose that I had been lonesome there or that I had hated to admit my ignorance when one of my relatives would ask curiously: "How do you say this and that in English?") I decided to learn to speak English. I began to read the local English newspaper, then some reviews and magazines. One Saturday evening, I remember it was a soft spring night, I ventured to go to the public library. You may believe is was quite difficult at first; I had to resort often to the French-English dictionary. After a while, it became clearer, easier; and what a great feeling it was to understand what people were saying in the streets, in the stores, everywhere!

Then my first child was born. I awoke to many new and unknown feelings, and I felt myself literally "taking root" here, if I may say so.

Some time before, I had read in the dictionary this definition: "*Langue maternelle, langue du pays où l'on est né* (Maternal language, tongue of the country where one is born)." I resolved that my children would know primarily the language of this country—their own. These children born and brought up in an English-speaking country must speak English correctly and without any accent; they must be permitted and not reprimanded for speaking English at home, not only with their playmates; they must be given good English books to read, so that their vocabulary will be constantly enlarged, so that they can penetrate the soul and know the works of the greatest Americans, who have made this country the greatest of all the world.

From now on, I looked forward; I was always proud of my French ancestry, but I "acclimated myself artificially." I did not wish to live in the past; you cannot go very far nor advance very fast if you look behind you.

There are things that you never know for certain. My father never said that he was sorry that he left Canada. He had a few thousand dollars when he died. He probably would have had as much, not in money but in property, if he had worked as constantly and as hard on his farm in Canada. And the feeling of loneliness, of being a stranger, of being nothing but an obscure cog in a gigantic machine, must have put a bitter taste in his mouth.

You know how Canadians love politics; some say they play politics *du jour de l'an à la St. Sylvestre* (from the first of January to the 31st of December). Well, he was never naturalized. My husband was one of the first to obtain the right to vote.

I think my mother was awfully lonely here. She never complained, but she lived her life watching for the postman.

I think sometimes that I would have had quite a different life, not better, not happier, but quite different, if I had married a Canadian *habitant*. But there must be a meaning to it; there is a meaning to everything that happens in life; only we don't always understand it.

We who are almost out of the picture are sometimes pleased to realize that we are still in the background.

Henri Lemay

When I was young, I wanted to be a *pilote branche*, a pilot who takes the helm and guides the transatlantic steamers up the St. Lawrence River to Quebec and Montreal. In the fall of 1881, I started from Deschambeau on the St. Lawrence River to carry a load of hay and grain to Lake Champlain. We went as far as Whitehall and then my brother, Tobie, and I decided to take the railroad train for Manchester where we knew we could find work in the mills. I had no intention of staying here. Yet I remained for twenty years before I even went back to my old home for a visit.

I was sixteen and Tobie eighteen years old when we arrived in New Hampshire. How lonesome we were at first! But soon we began to get acquainted with French-speaking people, and little by little, we became accustomed to our new surroundings.

The Manchester population was made up of Yankees, Irish and French at the time and there were no Greeks, Jews, or Poles in the city.

Oh, yes, we went to work in the mills. They were the big source of industrial life. At first I earned seventy-five cents a day and my brother fifty cents and, though you may not believe it, we lived frugally but decently on these wages. You see, we could buy good steak for twenty-five cents; chicken cost twelve cents a pound; a soup bone with much meat on it was only four cents a pound; and eggs were three dozen for a quarter of a dollar! No meat came from the West and there were four or five slaughterhouses in the outskirts of the city.

Two or three times a week cattle going to the Brighton stockyards were driven down Elm Street, and men were hired to stand at the corners of the side streets to keep the animals in line. All the public parks and private properties on the route were surrounded with iron or wooden fences to protect them from straying cattle.

Except for an oil lantern or a small gas light here and there, the streets were not lighted at night. I remember very well that I bought a pretty little kerosene oil lantern to carry on my arm. How bright and shiny it was! And it was very handy to go home after an evening when I *aller voir les filles.*

More than once I made a hit with this little lantern when I brought the girls home after a *soirée dansante,* where we danced the cotillion and square dances.

Oh, yes, the parents objected more or less about letting young people go dancing. *M. le curé* was very much against it, but we arranged to go just the same! The girls told their mothers about it only the day after, you see! But no harm was done. We were not as "excited" as the young of nowadays, but don't forget that we were hard at work from six o'clock in the morning until six o'clock at night!

We French people kept together and made our own good times. Every Sunday evening some five or six people assembled under one roof, living up to the old saying, *les amis de nos amis sont nos amis.* They were pleasant, those meetings.

You ask how we French were accepted in Manchester. Oh, yes, we must admit the Yankees and Irish did not like us. No, they did not like us at all! They appeared to bitterly resent our coming here. Not more than twenty years ago a good friend of mine, a genuine old Yankee with whom I have had frequent business dealings and political contacts then and whom I always see with pleasure now, said to me: "I like you, Henry! You're a good fellow! Not exactly like the other Frenchmen I have known here! Are you sure you're pure French?" I assured him that every drop of my blood was of French extraction.

After a few years in the mills, I began to grow dissatisfied and felt that I should learn some kind of trade. By this time my parents, two sisters, and a younger brother had followed Tobie and me here. We lived in a block where there were six other French families and in our few spare hours we had gay times together. We all worked hard but lived comfortably.

The girls earned from fifty to seventy-five cents a day. Each had her "best dress" made of fine wool and trimmed with bits of velvet, silk or lace for Sunday, and she always managed a new hat for every other season. Girls wore very high boots, and I remember that once when I had a job in a shoe store I sold a pair of shoes with twenty buttons to a young lady one Saturday night!

All the time I was looking about for a trade to follow and finally I hit upon the idea of becoming a clockmaker. That was a good move on my part for I came to like the work, and having a flair for it, began to make a good living.

I now became interested in politics and occupied minor posts which made me aware of the importance of civic institutions. I became a citizen in 1887 and have been active in the associations which take care of the naturalization of newcomers. Now they come no more from Canada for the government has awakened to its mistake of allowing so many French Canadians to become citizens of the United States.

I bought this house about thirty years ago. When Webster School was laid, a man named Martin bought several houses which had been built around here right after the Civil War and which were inhabited by veterans. He made cellars and dug wells on this street and the houses were then transported and set upon them without mishap. You can realize how old these houses are if you look at the next one on the right side. It is just as it was then.

I entirely renovated the inside of my house and installed plumbing and central heating. The well in the cellar has been filled up; my wife was always afraid that I'd fall into it. The outside has been refaced in crushed stone; but still the same old house.

Mike and Catherine Pelletier, probably in the 1930's, and the accordions with which they entertained themselves and their friends at home and at a wide variety of social occasions.

The Morin brothers in front of their fruit store in Old Town, Maine, in 1922. From left are: Frank, Clement, Joseph, Lawrence Sr., and Lawrence Jr.

Old Town, Maine

If French-speaking Canadians were lured to Manchester by work in textile mills, they came to Old Town for work in lumbering. By the 1830s, that city had become the jumping-off place, not only for Henry David Thoreau's travels in Maine, but for all the woods workers of the Penobscot river watershed. It would remain that for most of the next one-hundred years.

Through most of those years, Old Town would appear to be a place of sawmills, originally powered by a dam across the Penobscot River. In the winter months lumbermen from Old Town and elsewhere would chop or saw down pine, spruce, fir, and hemlock all along the tributaries of the Penobscot. They would trim the branches and haul the logs by horses or oxen to the landings at the edge of lakes or streams. Each log was marked by ax with the distinctive "brand" of its owner. When the ice went out of these lakes and streams in April or May, the great piles of logs on the landings would be pushed into the water and driven and floated down the streams and into the Penobscot. Just upstream from Old Town all these logs were gathered at the Argyle and Pea Cove Booms where several hundred men spent the summer and fall sorting them by "brand" and combining the sorted logs into rafts for further floating to the 100-200 sawmills which lined the river from Old Town to Bangor and Brewer, and on to Hampden. In the 1890s, these sawmills still sawed an average of 200,000,000 board feet of lumber each year.

Given its relatively small population, Old Town's economy continued to be fueled by woods industries—the Argyle Boom, sawmills, box factories, and suppliers of goods and services to the industry. Throughout the nineteenth century Old Town's boosters hoped that the city's water power could make it the Lowell of the Penobscot, but it got only two small woolen mills in the 1880s and 1890s. The same period brought a major paper mill in the Great Works section of the city and two canoe companies which would continue to provide employment for the city's people long after the boom, sawmills, and woolen mills had shut down forever.

Old Town's sawmills and woods work originally attracted a Yankee and Irish population rather than French-speaking Canadians. Of the city's 3395 people in 1880, only fifteen percent were Franco-Americans. By 1900, one-third of the city's 5765 people were Franco-American, but most of these were still new arrivals and transients. A Catholic parish census of 1903 indicates that 1260 of approximately 2000 Franco-American parishioners had lived in Old Town less than ten years. From then on, however, the Franco-American population stabilized and remained about one-third of the total. Already there was a small collection of French-speaking merchants. Most of the other merchants had at least one French-speaking clerk to attract Franco-American shoppers.

This sudden rise in the Franco-American population in the last twenty years of the nineteenth century was facilitated by the completion of railroad service between Maine and the Maritime Provinces of Canada. French speakers from that "new Acadia" of New Brunswick's Gulf of St. Lawrence shore and the valley of the St. John River and from the Riviere du Loup-Rimouski region of Quebec could easily reach Old Town by rail, as they did.

Once in Old Town, most Franco-Americans settled on an island which came to be called "French Island" and was connected to downtown Old Town by a bridge. The original homes were often little more than shacks, made of sawmill waste. Soon these were replaced by small, single-family houses with small gardens set close to each other. By the 1890s French Island population growth required that town government build new streets, expand the island's public school, and improve the bridge. A steel bridge was erected in 1913. By the 1930s, according to the Federal Writers' Project worker, "the French who live on French Island are apt to resent any disparaging remark concerning the place, but many of those who have moved to other sections of the town sometimes feel superior to those living across the bridge. A French women who lived in this part was telling a friend and me about what a nice home some newly married couple had acquired. She described the place in glowing terms but added, 'Of course, you know, it is on the island.' "

A Catholic parish, largely Irish, had met since 1852 in a small wooden building. By 1903 the parish had become French, operated a bilingual convent school, and had erected a large brick church, St. Joseph's. "To satisfy the church goers who understood no French," wrote Robert F. Grady of the Federal Writers' Project, "the assistant to the pastor was usually Irish. The pastor was always French and often people who couldn't understand that language had to sit through a sermon delivered in a foreign tongue. Dissatisfaction increased among these people after one of the Irish priests, who was transferred, was replaced by a Frenchman, and the proposal to create a new parish and erect a new church found favor." Indeed, in the 1920s, a new church, St. Mary's, was built just one city block away from St. Joseph's with services in English. "Shortly after it was completed many of the French who objected to what they referred to as the grasping tactics of the pastor of St. Joseph's, deserted that parish and joined St. Mary's. The Irish of the latter church offered no objections: they were satisfied so long as they had an Irish priest and sermons in English."

French-Irish conflicts were not always resolved that easily. In 1872, fights between French and Irish workers on the Argyle Boom resulted in the Irish getting "a bad calking from the Frenchmen," according to a local newspaper, and required police patrols on the Bangor to Old Town railroad. Nor did such incidents end. Old timers, interviewed in the 1970s about their experience on the Argyle Boom in the first three years of this century, could still say that "the Bangor fellows was quite quarrelsome with the French fellows. The Bangor was Irish, see." As another witness put it, "the Bangor boys was a hard crowd."

Franco-American social life revolved around St. Joseph's parish. In the early days the big annual event was the "Coffee Party," a three or four day fund-raiser for the Sisters of Mercy with suppers, food, booths, and a different stage program each night, be it a play, minstrel show, or local vaudeville act. The event had been preceded by the selling of lottery tickets with the drawing held at the end of the "Coffee Party's" final performance. By the 1930s objections to the lottery, probably by Yankee "reformers," saw the "Coffee Party" replaced by the usual church carnivals.

By that time Franco-Americans had become more integrated into the mainstream of Old Town life. Their slight knowledge of English upon their arrival had restricted them to low-paid jobs as sawmill laborers and as woodsmen or river drivers. With the end of the sawmills and boom, they had moved on to better jobs in the paper mills, woolen mills, and box factories. Robert Grady estimated that in the Old Town Woolen Mill, where he had worked, 50% of the weavers were French. He further pointed out that all the WPA foremen, most of the sub-foremen, and two-thirds of the 150 WPA workers were Franco-Americans as well as a "high percentage" of workers in the stores and factories. At the post office two mail-carriers, one clerk, the porter, and the janitor were French. At city hall so were two of the three policemen, one out of four firemen, several school teachers, the overseer of the poor, and three members of the city council. Grady singled out for special mention Alec Latno, long-time mayor and shoe store proprietor, and George Desjardins, postmaster, owner of a harness repair shop, and long-time collector of taxes. Grady added that three of Desjardin's four sons and both daughters had attended the University of Maine. In addition to these, reported Grady, Franco-Americans operated three large grocery stores, four or five small ones, two wholesale fruit stores, two restaurants, six barber shops and four beauty parlors, three shoe repair shops, one drug store, two garages, two saloons, one undertaking establishment, and one monument works. Before needing the last two businesses, one could have been served by four Franco-American insurance salesmen and one Franco-American doctor. The occupations in this work history, however, were male. Old Town Franco-American women, unlike their Manchester counterparts, seldom worked outside the home.

Robert F. Grady, who gives us this information of Old Town Franco-American life in the 1930s and who conducted the interviews which follow, was not of French parentage. In matters other than language, however, he was very much like the Franco-Americans he interviewed. Like them, his parents had also come to Old Town from Canada, probably for the same reasons. He had gone to school with Franco-Americans, worshipped with them, and worked with them "in the woods, on the boom, and in factories." And, like many of them, the Great Depression found him on WPA. As a result, he added, "I think I understand them well enough to write something about them."

In taking down the testimony of Mike Pelletier and Alphonse Martin, Grady also provides us with two of the earliest, clearest, and most succinct accounts of woods work. Pelletier's account makes clear to even the uninitiated such esoteric and exotic woods terms as joint, beat, swamping, wangan, dingle, and jigger, as well as the mysteries of bean hole beans. He leaves out, however, a definition of "to soak," that is, to take a rest-break from working on a joint in a beat.

SOURCES

Library of Congress, Manuscript Division, WPA Federal Writers' Project, Folklore Project - Life Histories, Maine, "Noted French Canadian Personalities of Old Town as Remembered by Robert F. Grady," 13 pp.

Edward D. Ives, *Argyle Boom* (Orono: *Northeast Folklore*, XVII, 1977).

Old Town, Maine: The First 125 Years, 1840-1965, n.p., n.d.

David C. Smith, *A History of Lumbering in Maine, 1861-1960* (Orono: Maine Studies of the University of Maine at Orono, 1972).

Marcella Sorg, "Genetic Demography of Deme Formation in a Franco-American Population: 1830-1903," Ph.D. dissertation, Ohio State Univeristy, 1979.

Steve Comeau

Steve Comeau, French Canadian, was born in South River, New Brunswick in 1876. He is 62 years old. When he was very young his father moved to Kouchibouquac, which is also in New Brunswick. With the exception of some time spent in night school in Old Town, all of Steve's schooling was obtained in the town with the Indian name. He left Kouchibouquac in 1896 when he was twenty years old and went to Greenville, Maine. After staying there for six months he went to Waterville where he worked in a sawmill. For the next few years he worked in the woods near Greenville in the winter, and in Waterville in the summer. In 1901 when he was twenty-five years old he came to Old Town and has been here ever since. He worked in a woolen mill here as a weaver during 1901 and until 1906. From that year until 1910 he worked in Jordan's box mill. He went back as a weaver in the woolen mill next and worked there until 1912 when he went to work as an edger in Wing and Engle's box mill. He stayed there until 1917 when he went back to work in the woolen mill. Remained there as a night weaver until 1936 when the mill closed. Hasn't worked anywhere since. Has been trying to get a WPA job for a long time, but said they wouldn't put him on because his boy gets more than $14 a week in a plumbing shop. All the information I got from Steve was obtained before I told him it was for the WPA. He said if they couldn't give him a job he couldn't be expected to help them.

His wife was born in Petit Rocher. He has three boys and four girls. Two of the boys and two of the girls are married. The youngest girl is taking a commercial course in the high school. He is a Catholic and belongs to no lodges. Interest in his home and friends. Is of medium height. Has black hair, slightly gray, parted in the middle. Wears gold rimmed spectacles and is never without a pipe. Had all his teeth *pulled a few years ago but the loss doesn't show up much. Has a very pleasant manner and was always well liked by his fellow workers. Lost his home through foreclosure several years ago. Is well read and has decided opinions. Ought to tell a more virile story than any of the others I've seen so far.*

Robert F. Grady, Interviewer

I was born in Kouchibouquac in 1876. That would make me sixty two years old. That was just a little settlement—maybe two hundred people lived there. My father owned a farm of about 150 acres. Most of the people there owned farms, and they ran from 50 to 200 acres. Some of the folks up that way ran trap lines, and some of them worked in the woods in the winter and on the river drives in the spring. It was pretty much the same up there then as it was in Maine about that time. Some times people up there would go across the line to work in the Maine woods in the winter, and go back to work their farms in the spring. There was practically no business or industry of any kind in the place I was brought up in. It was just a village of farms. There was a small Catholic church there. All the folks were French Catholics.

The school I went to had only one room and one teacher. I guess they had a grade system in the bigger places about like they have here. They always called the high schools "academies." I started going to school when I was about five or six and kept it up until I was twelve years old. I never had to carry any lunch because our farm was only about a fifteen minute walk from the school. The teacher was always a girl that boarded at one of the farmhouses. A few of the pupils that lived farther out had to carry lunches. I can't remember exactly what they had, but I imagine it was something like a couple of sandwiches made of home made bread and some fish, meat, or cottage cheese. It wouldn't always be the same, of course. They might have cake, cookies, or a doughnut to add to that. There were a lot of things they could carry such as a tomato, a piece of pie, or an apple. They carried tea or milk to drink and unless there was a fire in the stove they had to drink it cold for nobody had any vacuum bottles then.

Living conditions up there when I was a boy were a lot different than they are now. Of course, I'm talking about the small villages like the one I lived in. They didn't have any telephones, bathtubs, washing machines, electric lights, radios, or a lot of things people think they have to have today. We used to have dances and parties, but nobody ever thought of a moving picture show then. I think, though, we enjoyed ourselves just as much as people do now.

The fuel was always wood, and there wasn't anything automatic about it. Some people had a pump in the kitchen, but usually it was out in the yard. Instead of raising just one crop the farmers went in for general farming. They raised about what they needed, and although they generally had plenty to eat, they never had much money. There were no laborsaving machines on the farms up there then. Nobody sprayed apple trees, and grain was treshed on the barn floors. I don't think farmers worked any harder then than they do now. If you have tractors or machines that do the work faster, you simply go in for farming on a larger scale, so you keep busy anyway. The trouble with farmers nowadays is that they want to get a living without doing any work. If they'd work as long as people do in the factories they wouldn't be so hard up. When I was a boy on a farm in Canada I helped as much as I could with the work. Some of the farmers raised flax. The women would spin it into yarn and weave the yarn on hand looms into homespun cloth that was used in suits and overcoats. Winter stockings, winter caps, and mittens were always knit. We always kept enough sheep to provide wool.

I couldn't say much about the cost of living in Canada when I was young. About all we had to raise money for was shoes and clothing that we couldn't make, certain kinds of foods that we couldn't raise, and maybe a doctor's bill if we got sick. A lot of farmers had home remedies that were made from herbs to use for minor ailments. We never had to get money to pay light bills, water rates, fuel bills, etc. We could generally raise or grow enough extra to pay for what we couldn't produce. The more a farmer can raise the better off he is, for he has to sell his stuff at a wholesale price, and he has to pay a retail price for what he buys. Sometimes when a couple of the young folks got married a lot of the people would get together and help build a home for them. The roads were always pretty bad in the spring, but they were all right at other times. In the winter people had to travel in sleighs or pungs, and if the day was real cold they had to dress pretty warm to keep from freezing. Unless you had hot bricks or something like that to keep your feet warm it was like sitting with them on a cake of ice.

The French Canadians that came to Maine about the time I did, didn't come from any special section of Canada: they came from all parts of it. I guess, though, that the most of them came from Quebec. Quite a few came from Nova Scotia, New Brunswick, Prince Edward Island, and the Province of Ontario. The people from New Brunswick, Nova Scotia, and Prince Edward Island could generally speak English pretty well, but you could tell they came from Canada by the way they talked. It used to be an awful insult to call anybody a P.I.

There were different reasons why they left, I suppose. When a person leaves one place and goes to another, the main reason why he leaves is because he wasn't satisfied in the first place, and he thinks he can better himself by going somewhere else. I know a lot of people up there were hard up. They thought times were better in the States, and I guess they were. Some of the farmers thought they could do better farther south in Maine where the growing season would be a little longer. Some of the young fellows, like myself, couldn't see much future for themselves on a small village farm where there were a lot of kids growing up. Some of them wanted a change, or they wanted to see a little of the world. The ones that left were generally of the poorer classes, and they thought they could do better across the line.

In early days there were no restrictions whatever on immigration; that is, there were no laws or regulations to prevent anyone from coming to the States from Canada. There may have been family objections in a few cases, but they were seldom serious. The greatest obstacle was generally a lack of the necessary cash. Some of those that left were fortunate enough to have relatives here that they could stay with until they found work. I think the first immigration laws were passed soon after the Aroostook War, but for a long time they weren't strictly enforced. The laws have been changed from time to time, and a head tax has been added. The laws are strictly enforced now, and the quota can't be exceeded.

I left Kouchibouquac in the spring of 1896 when I was twenty years old. My folks were in their fifties then. They didn't exactly like to see me leaving, but I had some brothers of near my own age who could carry on the work on the farm. My father said that maybe I could better myself, but that if I couldn't, I could always come back to the farm.

They sold fruit, sandwiches, and candy on the train, but I didn't buy any for I had a little lunch wrapped up in a newspaper that I had brought from home. The trains then ran along pretty fast as they do now. It takes about seven hours to go from St. John, New Brunswick, to Bangor these days, and they used to make the trip in about eight hours fifty years ago. The railroads charge two cents a mile now, but when I came here the fare was between three and four cents for a mile. People going on trips then could save a fraction of a cent on a mile by getting a mileage book. These books had little tickets in them. If you travelled fifty miles the conductor tore out fifty tickets. They were supposed to be non-transferable, but brokers handled them, and you could get a book, or part of one, use as much mileage as you needed, and return the book to the broker. Pawnshops sold them, too, with various amounts of mileage left in them. The tickets were no good if they were detached, and the conductor always took the covers when the last ticket was used. Brokers stopped handling them about twenty-five years ago when fares were reduced so that there was no profit for them in selling mileage.

I had earned enough swamping in the woods the winter before to pay my fare to Greenville, Maine and leave me about thirty dollars over.

I didn't feel so bad when I left home, but when I got to Greenville that night and found myself among strangers, I felt pretty homesick. I worked in Greenville for about three months and then went to Waterville where some cousins of mine lived. For the next five years I worked in Waterville except in the winters when I went up in the woods near Greenville to work. In 1901, when I was twenty-five years old, I came to Old Town, where I've been ever since.

The French Canadians who came to Maine either went to some town where they had relatives, or they started for some place where they thought they could get the kind of work they could do. The towns that had large French populations were pretty well known, and they naturally attracted the most immigrants.

Maine, or the States, was the logical place for anyone in eastern Canada to come to if they were looking for a better place to live. It was no use going farther north, nobody wanted to cross the ocean to go to some foreign country, and western Canada wouldn't have been much of an improvement over the eastern part. Just how many came over in any of the last fifty years would be hard to say. Maybe the immigration people could tell you. Only a certain number are allowed to come in every year, and I guess there is always a waiting list.

There weren't many who went back to Canada, summer or winter, once they got here, I can tell you that. Some of them may have gone back because they got discouraged or homesick, but they were exceptions. The majority of the people who come here intend to stay. They like to go up on vacations sometimes, but these trips are usually taken in the summer months. When Father Trudell, a former pastor of St. Joseph's Church, was alive he used to run excursions every year to St. Anne de Beaupré, and a lot of French people went up on those. I never went up on one of those, but they say a lot of people get cured up there. I've heard there is a big pile of crutches just inside the door where they were thrown by people who didn't need them any more.

The average age of people who came over would be hard to say, but I think it would be in the early twenties. More men came over than women. The women were generally unmarried, and they usually found jobs in hotels or with private families, unless they had some special skill. Some of them that had experience in textile mills or shoe factories, got work along those lines. I know a lot of whole families came over. Look at the Morins. They came to Old Town about the time I came to Greenville. Including the old folks there were about twenty-five in the family, and about all they had was the clothes they were wearing. They tell me Frank used to go around barefoot because he didn't have any shoes to wear. Frank and Lawrence started a little fruit business in a tent about where the Morin store is now. Lawrence was pretty shrewd, and Frank was well liked. He was real polite, and he made the customers feel that he was tickled to death to see them whether they had only one cent to spend or a couple of dollars. He always managed to look clean and prosperous even when he was getting started. Before the chain stores came to town the Morins had a regular monopoly of the fruit and confectionery business in Old Town. They did wholesale and retail business. A few years ago they were rated among the richest people in town, and for a long time Frank was called the best dressed man in Old Town—I guess he is yet. Lawrence is dead now, and Frank has sold out and gone into the real estate business. I guess the way to get ahead is to have a lot of people going around telling what a good fellow you are. I wish I'd known that fifty years ago.

Mr. and Mrs. Ovide Morin

Ovide Morin, Sr. has a wife and eight children—all boys except two, and all married except two of the boys. Three of the boys operate the O.G. Morin wholesale and retail fruit business. They deal in fruit, candy, ice cream, cigars, etc., and own much real estate in Old Town including the brick block which houses their business, and doctor's offices on the floor above. They make a high quality ice cream. Mr. Morin had very little schooling, but reads French and speaks English with a noticeable accent. Vocabulary is not extensive. Is very intelligent. Has worked on the river, in sawmills, and as a carpenter and a brick and stone mason. Catholic. Lives next to his married son, Ovide, Jr. Both houses are good. Mr. Morin's house is very clean inside and is tastefully and expensively furnished. He is about 5 feet 6 inches tall, tanned, of wiry build. Hair is thick and iron gray, and his brown eyes are bright and alert. Appears to be in his fifties rather than in his seventies. Has a wide mouth that seems to be a characteristic of this branch of the Morin family.

Wife is an extremely attractive woman in looks and manner. Seems to be younger than her husband. Has remarkably attractive hair—white, wavy, and very "alive" looking.

Probably Mr. Morin himself did not save very much, but his sons, who started and who operate the O.G. Morin business, are among the wealthy men of the town. They are all very pleasant to meet.

R.F.G.

Mr. Morin: "Well, I don't know what I can tell you. I don't speak English very well, and maybe my wife could tell you more about things. If we could speak in French—"

Mrs. Morin: "Oh, you can talk well enough to tell him what he wants to know."

Mr. Morin: "Well, I was born in 1862 in St. Epiphané—that's what it is in French—can you handle that all right?"

Mr. Morin: "St. Epiphané was just a little place. I couldn't say how many people lived there. Yes, it was about as big as West Old Town (150-200 population). There was only a little church there and a little school. Just a lot of farms there. My father helped to build that church. He was a carpenter and a stone mason and a shoemaker. Sometimes when he had a small piece of hide left over he would make a pair of moccasins for some child who had nothing to wear on his feet. Sometimes there were children up there who had to go barefoot in the winter time."

Mrs. Morin: "Do you know there are some places in this country, near Fort Kent and the border, where conditions are about the same as they were in Canada then. The children have nothing to wear on their feet in the cold weather; sometimes they have little to eat and no money to buy anything. They have tables made of three boards nailed to the wall, and all they have for chairs are benches made of wood like you see sometimes. Those places are off the line of travel, and people don't see much of them. It is terrible that such things should be, and it is too bad that something can't be done about it."

Mr. Morin: "Some farmers can take a load of vegetables, grain, or fruit to the big city and bring back money from the sale of their produce. But they have to have money first to buy horses, tractors, or fertilizer. It takes money to make money, and those poor people haven't any.

"Conditions were very bad up there. Mister, what would you think of anyone who had to work a month to get $5.00—and sometimes you had a hard time to get the money, at that. 50 cents a day was big pay. When I was young I worked sometimes helping farmers pick their potatoes. One man offered me 25 cents a day if I worked for him. We worked from four o'clock in the morning until six o'clock at night, and then the farmer put us down cellar storing the potatoes until twelve o'clock at night. I told him I'd work for twenty-five cents a day, but I wouldn't do two days' work in one. I told him he hired me for twenty-five cents a day, and if he wanted me to do two days' work in one day he'd have to pay me fifty cents. He says, 'Oh, come on. Get through with the job and I'll pay you twenty-five cents extra when we get done. But I wouldn't do it, no sir. I wouldn't work two days for twenty-five cents.

"My father worked twelve and fourteen hours a day. That was a little sawmill up there, and it had only one saw. The end of the log stuck up, and one man had a hold of the saw up above, and another man held it below. It was done by hand, and I've seen them saw enough slabs and boards that way to build a house. It was slow work. Do you know, Mister, there was a sawmill run that way with one handsaw right up here in Pea Cove, and not very long ago, either, no sir?

"What do you think, Mister, of a girl that worked a whole year for—what do you think—$2.00? Yes, she did housework."

Mrs. Morin: "We were up there on a visit some years ago, and I met that girl again. She was a woman about fifty years old then, and she was wearing a funny hat and funny shoes. I don't know whether you ever saw any like them or not. They had yellow metal plates on the toes. The metal went in around the sole and came up over the toe. Her hat had a very narrow brim and a very high crown, and she was wearing a homespun dress."

Mr. Morin: "She kept those clothes for forty years. She had just that one hat and the shoes. The people she worked for gave her a homespun dress every year. She got two dollars a year and she saved money on it."

Mrs. Morin: "We went to church together. When we came back we went up to her room, and she took off her hat and her shoes. She put the shoes away in a box, and the hat she put away *so carefully* in a tall hat box. She said it was the only hat and shoes she ever had, and she wanted to keep them as long as she lived."

Mr. Morin: "The girls wouldn't save much on two dollars a year now."

Mrs. Morin: "Well, they do spend too much. They were extravagant especially during the war."

Mr. Morin: "Every man had to keep the road clear in front of his farm. That was so they could get to church. There were fences on each side of the road and the snow drifted in there. Sometimes after a heavy storm it would take three weeks to get the road clear. You'd see men out there shovelling away. It used to drift back in again after it was shovelled out. Sometimes people had to go to church on snowshoes. I remember once when a boy was very sick and in danger of dying. It took a doctor three days to get to him from the nearest town on account of the deep snow.

"I don't remember that we ever had to pay taxes up there. If we did, it wasn't very much. Some of the people up there didn't have very much to eat. They got along on bread and pork, sometimes quite a while.

"I worked off and on for twenty-five cents a day and after five years of that I didn't have a cent to my name. When I was nineteen I told my father I was going to Maine. I wasn't going to work all my life for nothing, and I knew I could get a dollar a day in Maine. My father says, 'My boy, I guess you're right. We'll pack up and all of us go to Maine.'

"I didn't work in the sawmill when I first came here—I worked on the boom. I worked out around the farm in Pushaw for nine months before I worked anywhere else. That old man, my father's cousin, lied to my father when he came up to Quebec. He told him that the farm in Pushaw was a good one and that it was big enough for all of us. He was getting too old to work it, and he wanted us to help him. The ground was no good; it was all clay. Some places on that farm hadn't been plowed in fifty years. The hay grew some places only a foot high. The next spring I went up on the boom at Pea Cove and from there I went to Argyle.

"I couldn't speak a word of English when I got there. No, I didn't have any trouble getting a job or getting along with the others. You see, there were so many French. There were a lot of sawmills here then. I got a job in Barker's mill. I told the boss when I went there I couldn't understand English, and he says, 'That's all right, I speak French, and all you got to do is understand me.'

"I worked in the sawmills, in the woods, and on the boom. When I went to work on the boom they paid the people who didn't know much about the work 75 cents a day. The old hands got a dollar a day. We got our board, too.

"Gene Mann was the boss then—you remember him? And how he could stay on a log! I've seen him jump on a log, kick the wedge out and roll it across the stream.

"One day I hollered out, 'Hey, Gene! Would you like to have me out there with you?'

"He looked over and kept right on rolling the log.

" 'Would you like to get wet, my friend?' he says.

"I could never stay on a log. I never learned how.

"One day Gene was going by where I was working and I says, 'Look here, Gene. I can do this work just as well as those fellows over there, can't I?'

" 'Sure you can,' he says.

" 'Well, how is it,' I says, 'I get only 75 cents a day while they get $1.00?'

" 'What!' says Gene. 'You mean you get less than they do?'

" 'The timekeeper just went by,' I says, 'and he told me I was getting 75 cents.'

" 'I'll speak to that timekeeper,' Gene says. 'Don't you worry any more. You'll get just what those fellows get.'

"Yes, he was a fine man—all those Mann boys were.

"Some of those fellows certainly could stay on the logs. I was down near the river here one day, and a fellow came along that wanted to get on the other side. There was just a log there that had been in the water a long time, and it was pretty well watersoaked. That fellow took that log and rode it across the river. He was in the water up to his waist all the time. I don't see how he did it.

"When the work stopped on the boom, I went to work in the sawmill. I worked there just one year. I told you my father was a mason. I went to work with him after I left the mill, and I never went back. Of course, some winters when there wasn't much work, I went up to the woods.

"I worked on St. Joseph's, the new brick church down here. I was doing rough work and one day the boss came around and says, 'Morin, your father was a good brick mason. I haven't got enough masons. Can't you lay bricks?'

"I told him I built lots of chimneys, and I probably could if he wanted me to.

" 'All right,' he says, 'come over here and start on this corner.'

" 'I can't do that,' I says, 'I can lay bricks along the wall, but I can't work on that corner.'

" 'Gwan,' he says, 'I got it all marked out for you. Go over there and lay those bricks.'

"Well, I built it up five feet and I stood back and looked at it, and it was just as straight as a die. After that I called myself a bricklayer. My father and I took a lot of jobs after that—all big ones. When we got done on one job we never wasted a day— we started looking for the next one. We never went out of the state, but we did work in Lewiston, Portland, and places like that. Once we went up to Van Buren on a job. What really made O.G. Morin was the Bangor fire. We had work there for five years. That fire pretty near wiped out the business section, and they wouldn't let them build with anything that wasn't fireproof. It's hard for me to remember where I worked any certain year. It's not like working in a mill—you're changing all the time. I can't remember what year the Bangor fire was, but I think it was in 1911.

"I couldn't tell many good stories about laying brick. When anybody's working at that job, they don't see much of what's going on, and when they get through at night they're tired, and they just go home and sit around awhile and then go to bed. Just the same, I worked on some of the best brick buildings in the town, and sometimes I go over there and look at them. They're just as good as ever.

"People got $14.00 a month in the woods when I came here, but if they lost a day on account of rain, they'd get the same pay. They get more money now, but if they lose any time, they take it out of their pay. People got $1.25 a day then in the mills. There wasn't much change in working conditions until just before the war. We worked twelve hours a day in the sawmill, and just before the war I think they had a nine hour day. They kept cutting the hours down from twelve until they got them down to nine, but the pay didn't go up very much until the war. We worked eight hours a day laying brick, never more than nine hours. That's long enough. They say a man will lay as many bricks in eight hours as he will in twelve, and I believe it. They got better pay during the war, but it cost more to live. You could save money, though, if you weren't foolish enough to throw it away like a lot of them did. Some people bought houses then or put their money in the bank, but some of them bought a car and in five years they didn't have anything. They thought good times last forever, but I'll bet they're sorry now.

"When I started to work in the sawmill, I moved over here to French Island. We had five rooms and we paid $3.00 a month rent, but of course that was just a shack."

Mrs. Morin: "It was *not* a shack! It was a good house. It would cost $10.00 a month, now."

Mr. Morin: "Well, maybe it wasn't a shack, but it wasn't very good. Do you know, Mister, the women used to go across the river and pick up waste slabs from the sawmill to build houses. There was a sawmill right across there on the Old Town side of the river. Yes sir, they built shacks with those waste slabs to live in. That, of course, was before I came here—I just heard about it. The sawmills don't throw away those slabs now—they cut them up into four foot lengths and sell them for wood.

"I guess conditions have changed a lot. In the first rent we had here we didn't have a table like this. We had some boards hinged to the wall for a table with just one leg to hold it up. The children had boxes to sit on. I tell you, Mister, I rather be dead than go back to those days. It was forty-nine years ago when we got the water here. I can't remember when we got the lights."

Mrs. Morin: "We were married forty years ago, and I'm sixty-five now. I've never been able to get my birth records."

Mr. Morin: "You ought to take a few years off your age then."

Mrs. Morin: (Not minding the interruption) "There wasn't any resident priest in Old Town then. A priest went around to four different towns: Orono, Old Town, Milford, and Bradley. When a child was baptized, the parents had to take it to wherever the priest was at that time. I don't know where they took me. It might have been in any one of those four places. I never could find the records anyway. I think that priest was Irish in those days. He couldn't pronounce the French names very well, and they said when he got one he couldn't pronounce at all, he baptized the child something else.

"When I was about two years old they had black diphtheria here. That was sixty-three years ago. Doctor Norcross was the doctor then. There were four children died in our family, and one of our neighbors over there, lost six. My mother got Doctor Norcross one night for one of my sisters. He put some white powder on the end of a knife and poured it down the child's throat, but in the morning she was dead. There wasn't much sanitation over here then, and a lot more children used to die. It wasn't black cholera that time—it was black diphtheria. That's what the doctor called it. If they had black cholera here, it was before my time. It must have been terrible to see so many children die. Once when I was six years old I got a sore throat, and my mother was afraid it was diphtheria. She got Doctor Norcross, and he asked if I ever had black diphtheria, and my mother told him I had had it. 'Well,' he said, 'don't worry then—this is just a sore throat.'

"I lost just one of my children—my little girl. She was eight years old, and she was a dear. For a time I hated everything because she was taken from me.

"I used to have dreams. I would be sitting here in the kitchen, and I would see her. She would walk by me carrying that great, heavy cross, and I couldn't help her!

"One day the priest said to me, 'Mrs. Morin, you feel bad because you hate your child! She is happy in heaven, and if you really loved her, you would be glad that that is so. A time will come when you will be glad that she is dead! Then you will really love her!'

"It was nine years after that when I was in the living room that I fell on my knees in front of her picture, and looked up at her dead face and cried. *I felt glad that she was dead.* I know that she is happy—far happier, perhaps, than if she stayed with us. I know I will see her again, for we all must die. I think of her often, now, but I never feel hate because she was taken from me. God knows best, and now I know that I really love her.

"A travelling man that one of the boys brought over to dinner once sat right in that chair and told me with tears in his eyes how he had lost his little boy. He said he had kept all the child's clothes. He felt so bad I felt sorry for him. How much better it would have be to give those clothes to some poor child who had none. I know that he didn't really love his child, or he would have felt glad."

Mr. Morin: "My folks were always good Catholics and we brought up our children that way. There are bad Catholics, but that doesn't mean there is something wrong with the religion. Our children have to be baptized, and when they get old enough they have to make their first communion. After that, they have to go to communion at least once a year at Easter time. Some of them go once a month. We don't believe in divorce, but sometimes people separate when they can't get along. There's more of that here than there ever was in Quebec."

Mrs. Morin: "Some people make fun of the Catholics for having fine churches when they haven't very good houses themselves, but there are a lot of worse ways to spend money. We think the church is the house of the Lord, and we think that house ought to be as fine as possible."

Mr. Morin: "The first time Father Trudel preached a sermon in the new St. Joseph's church he told the people, 'I didn't build this church for myself—I could get along with a pretty small one. I built it for you. It was your money that built it, and it will always be yours.'

"Sometimes we had a hard time to get to church in the winter time when we lived in Canada. We had to go through drifts or else go on snowshoes. They always kept the sidewalks plowed here, and now they plow the roads, too. People that live away out in the country can get into a warm car and drive to a warm church, and they don't have to worry about snow or cold."

Mrs. Morin: "We sent all our children to the convent. Nearly all French children went there then, but now a lot of them go to the public schools. There is quite a large one over here. Of course, the children have to go to the public school if they go to the high school for there is no Catholic high school here. The convent was not so big when we were married, and the sisters lived in one part of it. They built a big piece on about forty years ago, and when they built the new priests' house, they moved the old one up for the sisters to live in. That gives about twice as much space in the school.

"None of our children went to college, but two of the boys went to the business college for a while. Ovide, Jr. worked in his uncle's store for a few years before he started his own. Two of the boys work with him, and he has two clerks besides. They have a good trade because they really like people. They aren't friendly just because they think people are going to buy something."

Mr. Morin: "Mister, I think I made a good change when I came to Old Town. If I stayed in St. Epiphané my boys would have had to start just where I did. I'm glad they didn't have to go through with that. If they had stayed on the farm they would never have any money and no clothes to wear. It was plenty of hard work and nothing for it. Now they can dress well and they can live in a good house."

David Morin, Brother of Ovide Morin

Dave has a wife and six children, three of whom are boys, and three girls. One of the boys works as a drug clerk in a local drug store; one sells life insurance. Two of the girls are married. He went to Salem, Massachusetts, in 1883 and worked in a textile mill and attended night school. Returning to Old Town he worked in a box mill for twenty years, and then took over the management of a pool and billiard hall where candy, soft drinks, cigars, and fruit were sold. He became very ill with diabetes several years ago and was forced to retire. He looks to be in excellent health now and much younger than his sixty-eight years. Is a very good checker player and used to play pool and billiards very well. Attends the Catholic Church and is interested in local politics and world affairs. Chief interest seems to be in his home and children. Is about 5 feet 8 inches tall and dark-complected. Has deep-set eyes and prominent chin, and if his thick, iron gray hair were shaved off, he would look not unlike Signor Mussolini. Like most of the Morins, he was always well-liked. The store belonged to his brothers Frank and Lawrence. The Morins are all very pleasant people to meet—perhaps that is why they have done so well in business.

R.F.G.

I came here from Quebec in 1882, when I was twelve years old. There were twenty-five of us in the family. We had to sell our farm to get here. A cousin of the old man's—old Henry Martin, of West Old Town, you remember him?—wrote to us and asked us to come here and run his farm on shares. When we got here we found that if the farm had been in Quebec it would have been big enough to support two families, but it wouldn't here. Oh, yes, the ground is much richer up there. We couldn't all live off the farm, so some of us had to get jobs. I worked in the box mill twenty years before I got that job in the store.

There were no immigration laws when we came here. They haven't had those very long, you know. I don't know if the Bangor and Aroostook Railroad was running then or not. You see, we came in the other way, from the western part of the state through Danville Junction. I remember we were held up half an hour because the old man had fifty pounds too much baggage.

They used to go up to get them in those days. They didn't have people enough here to run the cotton mills and the factories. They used to go up there and offer people good jobs at good wages and their fare paid to any place they wanted to go. A lot of them went to Massachusetts. I worked in Salem in a cotton mill for a while. That's quite a city, Salem. A lot of them couldn't speak any English, of course. The boss used to use me once in a while as an interpreter. I remember once he came over to me and said, "Dave, you see that little girl over there—her name is Marie. She just spoiled a yard of cloth. Come on over and give her hell. Give her a good bawling out, and tell her it's coming from me."

I talked to her for a while, but of course the boss couldn't tell what I was talking about. If he had I probably would have got fired on the spot. When that son of a bitch got out of the way I helped her fix her machine.

I worked in Salem only six months. It wasn't only me—the whole family went. It was right after the sawmill shut down in the fall, and we all came back in the spring. If we hadn't rented our house for the winter we would all have come right back. We had the winter's wood in the shed, and we sold that to the family that rented the house. My father was a stone mason, and he couldn't find any work in Salem. He came back here with Ovide and Lawrence, and they all went up in the woods.

That was quite a big cotton mill in Salem where I worked. It burned down some years ago, but they built it up again on the old foundations. I think there were three cotton mills there then. There were about one thousand people working in that mill where I learned to weave, and they were nearly all French. They ran all the way from one to four looms—it depended on how much experience they had. I ran two looms. What they made it that mill was wide sheeting. I wasn't married then—I was only eighteen. If you go down to Salem you can still see that mill. I was back there just once since I left. My brother was going down in the car, and he took me with him. I stayed at my sister's for a few days down there.

When I came back to Old Town in the spring, I went up on the boom for fifty cents a day—including board—and I worked there all summer. That fall I had chosen to go up in the woods, for $13.00 a month, but my father said, "No, don't you take that, you can do better than that around here." I got a job in the box mill that winter, and I worked there until I got that job working for my brother in the pool room.

I don't think we had to pay any taxes on our farm when we lived in Quebec. Of course, I was only a boy when I lived there and I wouldn't know much about that, but if they paid any taxes, they didn't amount to much. I remember everyone had to keep the road clear of snow in front of his farm. They don't weave their own cloth up there now. They send the wool or flax to some big place like Rivière-du-Loup, and they get back cloth. That is one of the biggest towns in Canada. It had a population of about 7000 when we lived in Quebec, and it's bigger than Bangor now. I was back there just once since I left. That was twenty-five years ago on a vacation trip.

Everybody in Quebec speaks French. I remember one night an old fellow came to the door. You'd call him a bum here, but we didn't call them that there. He couldn't speak French, but he showed us by signs that he wanted to stay all night and that he was willing to sleep on the floor. None of us was afraid of him. It was a rule up there never to turn anybody away. We got him something to eat, and when he got through with the meal my father showed him where he could sleep. He left after breakfast the next morning without us knowing anything about him. Can you imagine anything like that happening around here?

A lot of people who came to the States didn't intend to stay here. As soon as they had earned enough money to pay for their farms they went back to Canada. Some of them stayed here, and some of them came back again from Canada. When they come over here now they stay.

Conditions have changed a lot since we left there. We used to raise everything we needed. We raised flax and wool and spun them into yarn. We wove the cloth right in the house on a hand loom. We made everything we wore—shoes, too. They wore moccasins the year around—summer and winter. My father was a shoemaker and a brick mason. They heard he was a mason when he came to Old Town, and they used to come and get him to do mason work. Don't you remember when he used to go down to Bangor and bring back a hide and cut it up to make moccasins when he had nothing else to do?

The French are proud of their language. They speak only the purest French in Quebec. I went to school up there only a few years, but I went to night school in Salem. After they go to school up there a few years they study English. The people can read it pretty well, but they have a hard time to understand it in a conversation. French is all you hear up there. If a Frenchman comes down here and starts a business, he has to learn to speak English, and if anyone goes in business up there he has to learn French. It doesn't make any difference if he's an Irishman or a Swede. There are plenty of French in new Brunswick and Nova Scotia, and they're more apt to be able to speak English over that way. The French of Quebec must feel superior to the New Brunswick French. We call them Shediacs, but of course they don't all come from Shediac.

I took out naturalization papers twenty years ago. I hear they're rounding up the French Canadians that haven't, and they're sending them back to Canada. Serves them right if they don't want to be citizens.

When we moved down to Carrol Street they were all English around there, and I was afraid the kids wouldn't be able to speak French when they grew up. I says to my wife, "I'll make a trade with you: we'll speak only French in the house until the kids get big. Then they'll be able to speak it. They'll hear enough English outside." And that was all we ever did speak until the kids got out of school. When my boy Rudolph went down to the University of Maine he could speak English as well as anyone but he could speak French just as well. He took part in plays down there. My boy that works in the drug store over here says that knowing how to speak French has been worth a thousand dollars to him.

Morin is a very old French name. In France you see it over many shops. The Morins came to Quebec from France originally. We never attempted to trace the family back, but I know the Morins were of noble blood away back.

Did you see where the King of England is coming over here? No, I don't mean that visit: the paper says he's coming to stay. They claim they're getting ready for it up in Ottawa. That little island is apt to be an unhealthy place before long. Canada would be a much safer place to the king. England is apt to lose that island and all her colonial possessions in the Old World besides. Mussolini may conquer the Frenchmen, but he'll never conquer France. France will always be there.

My children were born here and brought up here. What would you call them? Are they French, or Americans, or Yankees? What is a Yankee, anyway? The Indians are the only real Yankees, if you come right down to it. Who else has a right to be called a Yankee? I heard a speaker down here a while ago talking on that very subject. He said that the French in Maine are just as much Yankees as anyone. Why not? Look back through the histories and you'll see that the French were here just as soon as the English. The only Americans here then were the Indians. Have the descendants of the English any more right to be called Yankees than the descendants of the French?

Ovide Morin, over there in the store, could tell you a lot about the early French. He's interested in that kind of stuff, and his father, Ovide Sr., ought to be able to tell you a lot more. He was older than I was when we left Quebec, and he would remember more about it.

Superstitions? Pooh! I haven't any of those. I've heard some of those common ones, but they don't bother me. My knife dropped and stuck in the floor the other day, and I said to my wife, "Someone's coming to see us." But I said that only for a joke—I didn't believe it.

There was something happened to me in the box mill once, though, that's as sure as I'm standing here. I ran a planer there, and you know how fast the belts go on that machine. There were some beams overhead, and there was a plank between two of them over the belt. We had to get up on the plank when we oiled the upper pulley. I got up there one day with the oil can, and I had just got my foot on that plank when I heard the words "Go Back!" The machines were making a lot of noise, and they were running around and singing and hollering down below, but there was nobody near enough so that I could hear the words as plain as I heard those, even if they had spoken them. I got down off that plank, and I happened to look up when I was putting back the oil can, and I saw that the other end of the plank was just hanging on the edge of the beam. If I had walked out there, when I got to the middle of the plank it would have sagged just enough to slip off the beam. I would have gone right into that belt, and you can imagine what that would do to anybody. Who spoke those words? It was nobody that worked in the box mill. You can't tell me that death is the end, for I know better. There is a lot that we don't see.

Of course, I've had some ambitions, but they were never very big ones. I never wanted much money—two or three thousand was all I ever wanted. I wanted to own my own house and to educate my children. I wanted them to have a better chance than us, and they've had it. I've done about all I set out to do, but a man's ambition is never dead. There is always something he looks forward to.

Mike Pelletier, Pulp and Paper Mill Worker

Mike Pelletier was born in Old Town, Maine in 1873. His father was born in St. Hubert, Quebec. Mike has lived in Old Town all his life and on the same street. Mike started in at the public school at the age of 5 in 1878, and transferred to the convent school in 1885. Finished his school education two years later in 1887. Mike is a Catholic. He is about 5 feet 10 inches tall and probably weighs 185 pounds, has good teeth, thick gray hair parted on one side, and is one of those fortunate men who never lose the enthusiasms of youth. He is a very interesting talker, is 66 years old, but looks to be 50 and acts as though he were 30. Both he and his wife look as though they get a lot of honest enjoyment out of living.

R.F.G.

My father lived on a farm in Canada. He came to Old Town from St. Hubert, Quebec, in 1865. He and his wife and their fourteen children came down from St. Hubert in a covered wagon something like the ones used by the old forty-niners. It was hooped and covered with canvas. You used to see one of those around here once in a while. They came down through Rivière-du-Loup, Edmunston, and Madawaska. I guess the reason father left Canada to come to Maine was because a lot of other people had left there, and he had heard that there were more jobs over here and better pay.

My father worked in different sawmills around here. One of them was built right across the river between the lower end of French Island and Old Town. All those rocks that make the current rough there are what is left of the foundations of that mill. It was burned thirty-four years ago. Shad Rips, on the Milford side of the island, got its name from the shad that used to run there. The people used to catch them with seines. The shad don't run there now because they can't get over the dams.

Father couldn't speak English very well when he landed in Old Town. The French Canadians never had any trouble getting jobs around here, though. There were a lot of French to help them out with the language, and a lot of the bosses were French. They got $1.50 a day in the sawmills in those days, and they had to work fifteen hours a day. There weren't any lodges or societies around here then—not for the French, anyway. After a man had worked fifteen hours a day about all he felt like joining was a mattress. There was no labor saving machinery in sawmills then, you understand. All the work was muscular. Nowadays logs are fed to the gang saws by automatic feed rolls, but in the old time sawmills they had to be "spudded" against the saws. They had to get their shoulders against the spuds and push for all they were worth.

They used rotary saws to cut dimension (2×4, 4×4, etc.), and gang and single saws to cut boards. The single saws were also known as "muleys." The gang saws and the muleys were vertical saws that ran up and down. They were moved by a wooden arm and crank arrangement that got its power from a water wheel. The lumber they sawed in those mills might have been used anywhere—across the road or across the ocean. It was sold to anyone who wanted to buy it no matter where he was located.

The people who worked fifteen hours a day in those sawmills had blamed little time or inclination to plant gardens, as you can well imagine. Twenty-five or thirty years later, when they had to work only ten or twelve hours, they began to raise a little garden stuff.

Wages were low then, but so were living expenses. You could get a rent for from three to five dollars a month, $2.25 paid for a cord of four foot wood, or you could go out here and cut stumpage for 35 cents a cord. You could get a barrel of flour for three or three and a half, and a quarter of beef or pork at four and a half cents a pound. The way those fellows did was to buy a lot of provisions to last them through the winter, and if they didn't want to go to the woods, they could sit back and smoke their pipes until spring with the chance that they could pick up a few odd jobs here and there while they were waiting for the mills to open in the spring. They would be broke when the winter was over, but they wouldn't owe anything—at least not very much—and they knew a job was in the offing.

About the only woods work around the State now is pulp cutting. The big stuff is all gone. When they used to cut that big stuff the head chopper would spot the trees ahead of the sawyers by cutting a little spot of bark off on the side that the trees were to fall. Then the sawyers would saw them down. Sometimes they'd get two or three logs out of one tree. The head swamper planned the direction of the roads, and swampers would cut the trees down as near the ground as they could. They'd throw the brush to one side and fill in holes in the road with short logs. The logs that the sawyers cut were hauled to yards and piled up there. One sled tender always worked with every teamster. After the logs were yarded they were hauled on sleds to landings near the brook or river that would carry them down to the boom in the spring. Woodsmen and log drivers worked from daylight 'till dark. The drivers had a longer day because the days were longer in the spring and summer. They slept in tents, and sometimes they rolled up in the blankets with their clothes wet. It was a hard life and men had to be plenty tough. They never had colds.

On those brook landings sometimes they'd pile logs right on the ice, and sometimes they'd pile them along the shore. I've seen logs piled fifteen feet high against two trees. In the spring they'd cut those trees down and let the logs roll into the water.

It was dangerous work. In the spring those logs were floated down stream from the woods during the spring drives and trapped in a jam at the Pea Cove Boom where the work of rafting began.

After I left school I worked on the boom until it closed in the fall. That was in 1887. I rafted logs all summer for fifty cents a day. A boom is a long line of logs tied or chained securely together end to end. The ends of such a boom may be tied to piers or to some point on the shore. A boom like this might have fifty different uses. It could be used to guide logs toward a mill pond, or to keep them from drifting out after they got there. However, when people used to talk of working on the boom they didn't mean a line of logs like that. By the way a "main boom," or double boom, was made to two lines of logs wedged together so that a man wouldn't have to be an expert to be able to walk along it. Two or three hundred men and boys have worked there when I did, but the number kept dwindling down every year until finally the work stopped altogether. There was a lot of logs piled up in a jam back of the gap, and a lot of different companies owned them. All the companies had their own marks and they used a different kind of mark for every kind of log; that is, pine, cedar, hemlock, and so forth. Those marks were cut on the logs up in the woods, and the logs were supposed to be rafted with the marks up. Those marks were something like the brands they put on cattle out west: Diamond rabbit track, flying goose, cross two notches, and so forth.

There was an opening in a boom in front of the jam that they called the "gap," and the logs were pushed down through that gap and rafted along a double boom they called the "shore

The rafting grounds at Argyle Boom on the Penobscot River. At right are shore logs and joints. The men on the river are checkers.

boom" or "shore logs" that reached down the river a half mile or more. All the rafters had to do was to raft the logs together with wedges and a rope. The checkers stood out on little jiggers made of three or four short logs wedged together and hooked with a short rope to a line that stretched from one end of the boom to the other. Every checker had his own "beat" and every beat was made up of "joints," or rafts. The checker rolled the logs while they were floating by him and pushed out the ones that were supposed to be rafted on his beat. The logs they missed were rafted in a "stray raft" at the end of the boom, and pulled back upstream when the raft got large enough. When the rafts on the different beats got large enough they were "dropped off" in a "swing." The men who handled the swings didn't do anything else.

When the small "joints" were combined in long rafts they floated down from the boom to the mills of the various owners. You might start down river to Bangor with a long raft, but if some of the logs were for mills in Old Town or Orono, all you had to do was kick out the wedges while the raft was floating along and shove the proper joints over to where the mill boom would guide them to where they were supposed to go. The gaps in the main raft would be pulling the sections together.

By the way, Mike, the boss asked me the other day what a "dingle" was, and I told him it was where they kept the horses in the woods. Later on I thought that was wrong. What about it?

If you'd ever taken horses to the dingle and left them all night, the boss would have explained what it was the next morning. A dingle is a storehouse for meats and provisions. You were thinking about the "hovel." The wangan was a kind of little store where tobacco, socks, mittens, thread, and stuff like that was sold. The timekeeper, who was also the clerk of the wangan, slept there, and there was always a spare bunk for the main boss. The cook had a bunk in the cook room where the crew ate its meals, and the blacksmith and the saw filer, the cook, the head chopper, the timekeeper, and the scaler felt superior to the common woodsmen, but if they were good fellows they tried not to show it. If a man was good, though, he was always respected no matter what he worked at.

I never saw any trouble or fights in the woods, but I saw a couple of bad accidents. They had men working around the blacksmith shop making sleds, and one of these fellows had a sled runner between his legs and he was hewing away at it with an ax when the ax slipped and cut his knee cap right in two. I saw another fellow get his leg crushed with a log on the landing. That was up at Brandy Pond, about 18 miles above Costigan. They had to haul those two fellows out to the railroad station at Costigan and from there they took them to the hospital in Bangor. There wasn't much they could do for those fellows in the woods except to do a rough job at setting the bone and put splints on the leg, but I suppose that had to be done over again when they got the fellow to the hospital. With that split knee cap all they could do was to bind it up to stop the bleeding, and get the fellow to Bangor as quickly as they could.

There were seventy-five men in that crew where I was. On rainy days they sat around playing cards—poker, for matches or beans, or high-low-jack. Sometimes they'd have some clothes to darn or mend, and sometimes they'd grind axes or make ax handles. I've seen as much as a barrel of ax handles ahead. They made some pretty good handles just with an ax and a jack knife and maybe a piece of broken glass.

To play poker if you didn't have any money you could go to the wangan and get a can of smoking or a plug of chewing tobacco. The banker in the game would give you ten or fifteen beans for that, and if you still had the beans at the end of the game, you could get your tobacco back. A bean represented one cent in merchandise. The men were supposed to boil their clothes every week or two on Sunday, but some of them didn't bother. We used to build a bonfire down by the brook, and put the underwear in a boiler full of water over the fire.

There was always someone that collected spruce gum. They kept it in a cloth bag. They'd make a dollar or two selling the gum to some drugstore when they got down river in the spring.

Beans were cooked in bean holes mostly on the river drives, but sometimes they cooked them that way in the woods. You see, on the drives the men were always on the move, and they couldn't very well carry a stove with them and keep taking it down and setting it up all the time. The cooks knew where those bean holes were along the shore, because they used the same holes year after year. All the cook had to do when the rear went by was to hop into a boat with his pots and pans and provisions and row down to the next bean hole.

We used to cook about ten quarts of dried beans a day for those seventy-five men, and that would be twenty quarts of cooked beans. The bean hole was about two feet deep and three feet square, but I've seen them four feet square. We lined the hole with rocks to hold the heat, and then we threw in some wood and got a good fire going. When there was plenty of hot ashes and coals in the hole we raked them away from the middle and set in the bean pot. Then we raked the coals and ashes back over the iron pot. That pot had an iron cover that fitted tight. We never had to add any water because that cover kept all the steam in. We filled the hole in with ashes. The beans cooked in about twelve hours and they had to soak about twelve hours before they were put in the hole. We used about a pound of pork to a quart of beans, and about a cup of molasses, to color the beans, to ten quarts.

The only fruit we ever had for the table in that camp was stewed prunes. We had salt cod and plenty of beef. Sometimes we had pea or bean soup or beef stew. We always had doughnuts, and sometimes the cook wouldn't use the bean hole; he'd just cook the beans on top of the stove in the iron pot.

Water Street in Old Town was a pretty wild place after the drives came in. Those drivers used to race down from the head of Indian Island. The redskins had a cannon over there and when that wild gang got in sight the Indians used to fire it off for a signal to the whites. A lot of people used to gather on the shore to watch them land. There were eight in a boat and when those boats hit the landing some of them would go nearly all their length up on the shore. The drivers made for Water Street the first thing, but they had to get by some people, like "Humpy" Mishou, first, that were trying to drag them in to sell them suits of clothes.

I've seen free-for-all fights going on on Water Street all the way back from the bridge down to the last saloon. Those fellows would get drinks and they'd start to remember words that had passed in the woods. Every word had to be accounted for. About all the police could do was to stand back and let them fight it out.

There used to be a sawmill in Great Works. It was right where the company power house is now. I've seen more than one driving boat go through that sluice and strike the white water at the other end. People used to go down there to watch the rafts go through; it was quite a sight. They used to think it was great sport to ride the rafts from Old Town down river to Bangor. People like the Smiths, the Rogers, and the Hinks, with plenty of money, used to bring lunches down in boxes and board rafts for the sail down river. Nobody objected, least of all the people who worked on the rafts. It was just good company for them. Going over the dam was where they got their biggest thrill. The rafts, of course, didn't go over the falls. They could have been broken up that way. The boats went down through the sluice, but the rafts went by way of the apron. The main part of the dam dropped off sharply and the current ran pretty fast through the sluice, but the apron sloped down very gradually. It was quite a sight to see the rafts of shipmasts go through. They were about seventy feet long, and of course they had to be rafted lengthwise. They used birch poles in rafting the shipmasts because they had to be careful they didn't break apart. There was a lot of money tied up in one of those rafts.

It wasn't only logs and shipmasts that were floated down. The sawmills used to make up rafts of dimension, and on those they would pile boards and smaller stuff such as clapboards, laths, and bunches of shingles. They were floated down to the docks in Bangor where they were broken up and loaded onto vessels. When the water was high early in the year they could make the rafts bigger and heavier. I've seen them 150 feet long and 50 feet wide. A raft of that size represented a lot of money.

On the dimension rafts that carried the smaller stuff, they used to bore two holes at the front end and drive in posts that kept an 8×8 from slipping off. This piece of timber ran along the front end and the boards were piled with one end of them resting on that. It had the effect of tipping up the front end. The rafts were steered with sweeps fourteen feet long and tapered up to a point at one end.

You used to see a lot of logs "hedgehogged" along the shore in the fall. Sometimes there would be as much as 10,000,000 feet ahead. Those logs stayed there all winter, and in the spring the mills used them to run on until the spring drives started to come in.

All they have now on the river is pulp wood drives, but they're nothing like the old ones. The pulp wood is cut four feet long and peeled in the woods. The boom is a thing of the past. Last year about 40,000 cords of pulp wood came down the river to Great Works, and 60,000 came by train. They haul it all the year around in trucks. They used about 500,000 cords last year. You see they have 50,000 cords in just one yard, and they have several yards down there.

When I quit work on the boom—or rather when it closed— I got a job in the pulp mill in Great Works. That was fifty-two years ago and I've been there ever since. I worked in the yard for five years and on the chipper for one year before I went inside. That mill was a pretty small place then compared to what it is now.

There was some of us standing around down there one day when Clapp was there. He was the owner of the mill and a millionaire several times over. He was looking at a dryer and he says to Wentworth, the superintendent, "I wish I could remember how long this dryer has been in here. I suppose I'll have to get them to go through the records in Boston to find out."

"There's no need to going to that bother, Mr. Clapp," I says. "That dryer was put there in the summer of 1889."

"H-m-m," Clapp says. "You seem pretty sure of your facts, young man."

"Yes, sir," I says, and I went on to tell him how long it took them to set the dryer up, who the boss of the crew was, and what they said it cost to do the work.

"Gosh," Clapp says, "there's no need of keeping records as long as you stay here."

I told him a lot more about different things in the mill he wanted to know about, and he copied it all down in a book. After that whenever he wanted to know anything about the place, he always came to me.

There was a *Bangor Daily News* reporter in there last summer. Wentworth was showing him through the mill, and they stopped in the evaporating room where I was at work. You must remember reading that interview in the *News*. That "grizzled veteran" that the reporter spoke about was me.

Wentworth says to me, "How long have you worked here, Mike?"

"Fifty-one years, sir," I says.

"Well, well," the reporter says, "that doesn't look as though they fire people who are over forty-five here!"

The evaporating room is where the water is taken out of the liquor that has been used in the digesters. When that reporter was in there last summer, Wentworth asked me to show him some of the water that was removed. I dipped some out in a dipper and handed it to the reporter.

"Why," he says, "it looks clear enough to drink. Do you mean to say this water came from the black liquid down there?"

"Yes, sir," I says, "the water has to be taken out before we can burn what is left."

That liquor is made up in the soda room and pumped to the digesters where it changes the wood chips into pulp. From the digesters the liquor goes to the wash room, then to the evaporating room and back to the soda room where it is used over again. You see, it keeps going around and around. During the evaporating process the carbon is burned out of the liquor, and the liquid that runs out of there to go back to the soda room looks just like molten lead.

There's been just three changes in the work in the evaporating room since I went to work at Great Works. When I started work there they used to burn the liquor by hand. Then they put in those three rotary burners. The automatic burner they have now is the best of them all. That new burner cost a quarter of a million dollars and it saves the company $5000 a week in operating costs. It produces 40,000 pounds of steam in an hour, so you can see there is quite a saving right there. In this new burner the fuel used is the liquor itself and that saves in fuel cost. It is only the carbon in the liquor that burns. The rest of it goes back, as I said, to be used over.

I've seen some bad accidents down there. Joe Gallant was down in the basement when a digester started to blow. The collar came off a valve, and the digester blew right in the basement room. When we cleared away that pulp, we found Joe on his hands and knees against the wall. His flesh was cooked so much that when we tried to pick him up, the flesh came off in our hands. You probably remember when old Henry Curran got his sleeve caught when he was oiling a shaft. Before they got the power shut off every bone in Curran's body was broken.

I was the oldest boy at home when I was growing up, and I helped quite a lot with the chores around the house. I shoveled paths in the winter, helped some in the garden in the summer, carried in wood, and brought in water from a pump in the yard. Father always raised some tobacco every year. Some of the leaves on those plants would be 18 inches long. He used to cut the tops off so the plants would spread out more. He started them in a hot bed so they'd have a little longer growing season.

When I was ten years old I used to go out in the woods with father to help cut the year's wood. We took our lunch and stayed all day. We'd build a fire at noon and heat up whatever we had. It was usually meat or egg sandwiches and some kind of pie or cake. We used to carry a bottle of tea that we'd heat up out in the woods in a big tin can that we kept for that. We cut ten cords every year—that's what we used in the house. What we cut one winter, we'd use the next.

I was twelve years old when I learned to play the accordian, and *Home Sweet Home* was the first piece I learned. I played the harmonica when I was ten. Father played the violin, and Lewis and George played the harmonica. Lewis played the accordian some, too. Some of those old pieces we used to play you never hear now, and I don't know where anybody could get them, if they could at all. There was *Peek-a-Boo, Rock-a-bye-Baby, Man in the Moon, Speed the Plow*, and a lot more like *Over the Waves,* and *Turkey in the Straw* that didn't die out.

    We used to have a lot of parties in those days, and we generally had a good time. The expense was so small that it wasn't worth mentioning. We used to play *Post Office, Spin the Plate, Play the Cushion, Catch the Rat, Blind Man's Bluff,* and *The Turn Over Game.* In that last one two of them used to lie down on the floor head to head and on their backs, lock legs together, and try to turn each other over. The girls used to play it, too. They'd wear bloomers or put on an old pair of pants, and some of them were pretty good at it. I've seen them turn some of the men over. *Spin the Plate, Blind Man's Bluff,* and *Catch the Rat* were kissing games. They'd take a plate and stand it on edge and give it a spin. If you could catch it without knocking it flat, you could kiss the girl, but if you missed the plate, you had to take a turn spinning it. In *Catch the Rat* they had a handkerchief tied up to represent the rat and you had to pick out the one that had the handkerchief. Everybody knows how to play *Blind Man's Bluff* and *Post Office.* In that cushion game they used to put a sofa cushion on the floor behind someone. The game was to sit down before someone could pull the cushion away.

    We used to have candy pulls, too, and molasses candy was a great favorite. They used a cup of molasses to a half cup of sugar, a little salt, some vinegar, and a spoonful of butter. After that cooked a while they set it on the back of the stove to cool off a bit, and then they stirred in some soda to make it foam up. Then they'd take it out and pull it until is started to harden up. Some people used butter on their hands during that pulling and some used flour. That pulling seemed to make the candy grainy and less glassy. It had about the same effect as kneading dough, I guess. Sometimes at those parties we had ice cream, and we always made it at home in a freezer; it wouldn't have seemed like a party unless we did.

    At those kitchen breakdowns we used to have whatever kind of music there was available. Somebody might have a fiddle, or maybe it would be an accordian of a Jew's Harp. Sometimes we sang songs. If there wasn't room for square dancing, we'd dance clogs. We used to have straw rides, too, but I guess they kind of went out when automobiles came in. About twenty of us—or ten couples—used to fill a hayrack with straw, toss in a barrel of beer, and set out for some farmhouse. I've gone on more than one of them out to French Settlement, West Old Town, or Pushaw Pond. When we went to French Settlement someone would go out around to all the farms and collect as many people as they could to join in the fun. We sang songs, danced, played games like *Post Office*, drank the beer and had a good time generally.

They don't have any of those straw rides and breakdowns now. They went out when the automobile came in. The young folks, now, go to dances and the movies.

We go to card parties once in a while, but I don't believe we've been to the movies twice in the last year. Those "love pictures" are no good, but I like a good Western. I don't read much now, but I used to like western magazines and stories. When I was a kid I never got enough of those Wild West yarns. In the *Bangor News* I like the sports pages and "smiles for breakfast." They have some good jokes there.

A few weeks ago we had a whist party over there in the convent to raise money for the school. Besides the card playing we had some moving pictures. There was a priest there from Lewiston, where Father Ouellette came from, and he had one of those home projectors and some moving pictures he'd taken in different places. There were some real good colored pictures of Montreal. One of the scenes showed a parade of priests. That was a narrow film, of course. The pictures on the screen were only about four feet square. But they were good.

When I was a kid I was too busy to have any ambitions. I had some younger brothers and sisters, and I had to help father to support them. When I got that job in Great Works, the only ambition I had was to stay right there as long as I could. Yes, I got this house, such as it is, and it's all paid for too. I own two lots across the street where my garage is, and I generally have a garden over there every year.

It's funny that I've lived here all my life, but my boys are scattered all over the country. That picture on the wall there is one of Rudolph, my oldest boy. He is in Missouri now working in a varnish plant. He was on a torpedo boat in the navy during the World War. He was over there when the German fleet surrendered to the British. That photograph on the piano is one of my youngest boy: he graduated from the high school last year. This year he is at a CCC camp. When the boys get finally settled, maybe they'll take after me enough to stay put.

I have belonged to the Catholic Foresters for the last thirty years, and my wife and I have been in the Grange for twenty-five years. When the Knights of Columbus got their charter here I was too old to be anything but a charter member so I never joined in. I have a life insurance policy in the Prudential, though.

Those accordians under the table belong to me and the wife. We played at WLBZ when that station first started, and maybe we'd be playing there now if it wasn't so far from home. Accordian music was something of a novelty on the radio then: people like it. We played at the first auto show in Bangor, and whenever the Grange has an entertainment, I guess they'd think it strange if we weren't there to play. Guess I've played the accordian for fifty years. If I gave you a list of the songs we played, it would be a long one. We could probably play all night without having to repeat anything. We always played the music of the day. Any music is good if it's played right at the proper time. I like all of it.

Mrs. Pelletier: Mike and I played over at the convent at a social Sunday night. That was given for Father Ouellette. We played the accordians, and there was violin and piano music. There was no dancing. There was some dancing, though, down in Hampden Monday night when we played at the Grange meeting. We didn't get home 'til four o'clock in the morning, and it was five before we got to bed.

Mike: That dancing was just to keep warm. I played the accordian for about an hour while we were waiting for the bus to come along and pick us up. There was about 300 Grange members down there, and I guess the feature of the evening was the clam chowder.

I mentioned that I had seen Mr. and Mrs. Pelletier's names in the paper after they had played at the Father Ouellette so-

cial, but that I didn't recognize the names at first because "Michael" was spelled "Magloire."

Mike: Well, my name is Magloire Pelletier. I suppose that sentence ought to be at the first end of the story instead of the last end, but it's better late than never. Mike is a nickname that they call me for short. My last name is Pelletier, but sometimes I spell it Pelkey. Mitchell is just the English way of saying my first name.

Mrs. Pelletier: I've always spelled my name "Pelletier." It's funny up on the voting lists they have me down as Mrs. Catherine Pelletier and him as Mike Pelkey.

Alphonse Martin, Woodsman

Alphonse Martin, born in 1901, was perhaps the youngest Franco-American interviewed in this collection. He may also be the only person from the Federal Writers' Project life-history narratives to be interviewed by folklore professionals in the age of the tape recorder. Between 1973 and 1976 folklorists from the University of Maine at Orono recorded five hours of interviews with him. His recollections, taped in the 1970s, about work on the Argyle Boom are remarkably consistent with the following account taken down by Robert Grady in the 1930s.

C.S.D.

Yes, sir, I worked on the boom maybe three to five summers. Gene Mann was the boss there. When I went up there for a job Gene said to me, "Can you stand on the log, my friend?" "Yes, sir," I told him, "if it's tied on both ends." Gene laughed at that, and he said, "Okay, my friend, I guess we can use you. Go down on the stream where the water ain't so deep, and tell Tobey—that's his boy—I sent you there." I went down there, and Tobey put me on the last joint of the first beat, and he said, "You go on there. Those hemlock don't run so fast today. Don't you raft anything but the diamond rabbit track." Tobey showed me how to raft the logs, and by and by I could do it just as well as anybody else. You grab the log with the pickpole and pull it over, and then you wind the rope around the toe and pull it tight. Then you put in the wedge and drive it in with the mallet. If that rope ain't tight enough you wind it around the mallet and pull on that and that makes the rope tighter. Those logs, you understand, have to be rafted tight. If they ain't, the logs turn over and you can't see the marks. One day I was sitting on the bank smoking a pipe when the hemlock weren't running so fast, and Joe Cote—he was the checker on that beat—hollered "Hey, Alphonse, sleep in the night time. Come out here and catch these logs. Do you expect me to go over and raft those hemlock for you?" He was joking, you understand. I tell you though, Mister, when Joe Cote got mad you better look out. That man fought in the ring sometimes, and he knows what it's all about.

One Sunday night a fellow came up from Old Town and he felt pretty good. "I can lick any son of a bitch in Pea Cove," he said. "Yowee!" Joe Cote lit a cigarette, looked at that fellow, and said, "You don't take in much territory there, my friend. Why don't you make that Penobscot County?" That fellow didn't like that because everybody laughed. He went over to Joe Cote, and he said, "Okay, smart guy, I can lick anybody in these parts. How do you like those apples, eh?" He made a big swipe at Joe Cote, but Joe saw that punch coming a long way away. He just tapped that fellow with an uppercut, and they had to wake him for breakfast the next morning.

Joe Cote was a great man for the joking. One time when it was his turn to soak, he hollered to me and said, "Come on, Alphonse, can you walk the shore log? Leave that pickpole there and those hemlock will raft themselves. Come with me and we'll get those strays." "Why don't you keep your eyes open?" I said, "and don't let these logs float past. Sleep with your hands outside the blanket." "Don't worry about Joe Cote, my friend," he said. "That's not the trouble. The rafters are dead from the ears up. They don't catch the logs when I shove them over."

We started back with that stray raft and Joe hollered, "Come on there, Alphonse. Bend that back. We ain't got all day to get those strays back." I pulled some more on the towline. Joe kicked the wedge out of its hole in the stray raft, and Alphonse Martin went into the water up to his ankle—with the head down. Joe laughed at that, but nobody got mad on the boom because his clothes got wet, for they dried in the sun in one half hour. I tried to put Joe in the water after that, but no, sir, I couldn't do it. He got most of the logs pushed out of that stray raft. The logs were pretty loose. When Joe stood with his back turned, on the log which had the towline, I gave that line a sharp pull. That didn't bother Joe; he just jumped to some other log. "Alphonse," he said, "when you can put Joe Cote in the water you will be much older than you are at present." I told you, Mister, it's pretty hard to put Joe Cote in the water. Gene Mann can't do that.

Something I never could learn was to ride logs. One time I saw a big one come by the joint. That log was a foot and a half on the butt. I jumped on top of that log, but it was a curved one, you understand. I couldn't see that because she rode low in the water. That log turned over very fast, and when those big logs roll over, they are hard to stop. Joe Cote pulled me out of the water, and he said, "Alphonse, you better stay on your raft. Then if you fall over you don't get wet."

There was a fellow there that didn't have much hair on his head, and one night when we played poker, someone said, "Onzime, the barber shaved you pretty close in the wrong place didn't he?" Onzime said, "My friend, did you know that was a sign of intelligence?" "If that's the case," the fellow said, "they ought to put you on the Supreme Court."

We don't wear many clothes on the boom in the summertime. Just a shirt, pants, and calk shoes. We don't stop for a rain there unless it's a pretty heavy shower. They wear greasers and slickers, and that keeps the rain off.

Lots of rafters can ride logs, but they don't have to. A checker, though, has got to be able to ride those logs. He stands on the jigger when he works, but if the log comes pretty fast he's got to get out there and work with both feet and the pickpole. I never wanted that job; those checkers get twice as much as the rafters, but they earn it.

That boom hasn't run now for twenty years. The long stuff has gone from this state for some time.

Vital Martin

Mr. Martin is 57 years old. Lives with his wife. Couple never had any children, but entertain a lot.

Worked on the farm and in the woods in Canada. Went to Lille (Maine) when he was 17 years old in 1898. Worked there 15 years mostly as a carpenter but sometimes in the woods. Moved to Old Town in 1913 and has remained here ever since. Went to school only two years in Canada between the ages of 6 and 8. The small house in which he lives and the large corner lot on which it stands belong to the church. He is janitor of the church. He takes care of the fires in the convent school, the sisters' house, the church, and the priests' home; shovels paths and keeps ice off the roofs. Mows lawns and does other work about the church property in the summer time. The job keeps him pretty busy. Is a very fast and efficient worker. Good carpenter. He never worked in a factory. Interested in local politics and local affairs. Is a Catholic. A little above medium height, slim, and dark. Has good teeth and a scar on his left eyebrow. Talks with a pronounced French accent in spite of his years in Maine. Smokes cigars.

R.F.G.

There wasn't any town where I was born in 1881. Just a lot of farms along the river, the St. John River. The nearest town was St. Leonards, but that was a small place. Just a few stores there and a sawmill, a church, and a small school. I don't remember much about the place. You ought to talk with some of the old fellows—75 or 80 years old. They remember a lot of stuff, and they talk right along.

There wasn't much work up there. They worked on the farm, in the sawmill, on the drive, and in the woods. They paid $12.00 to $14.00 in the woods when I was there. I remember my *grandpère* told me it's hard to work on the farm there. They have wooden harrows that they make themselves, and they plow the ground with a wooden plow that has something like galvanized iron on the point to make it sharp. Rich farmers that have money can get metal plows, but the poor ones have to make theirs themselves.

I remember once I helped a farmer harvest some oats. He had a wagon he made himself with two wheels on it and a rack to hold the oats. You can carry a lot of oats in one of those racks. He used oxen to haul the cart. By and by he put two more wheels on the wagon and made the rack bigger. That's the way they got started on the farms. They raised beans, corn, wheat, oats, and pork. We made our own clothes from cloth we made on the hand loom. I used to wear moccasins that my father made.

They can go hunting and fishing any time there because there was no warden. There was lots of wild game there and bears. Just one shot is all we needed to kill a bear. If we didn't kill him the first time, he got away for it took so long to load the gun. I remember my *grandpère* told me, "Vital, shoot the bear just once: that's enough to kill him." I never heard of anyone killed by mistake up there. I don't like to go out in the woods to hunt here, because it is too dangerous. You never can tell when someone will kill you for something else.

I wouldn't want to go back there, though. This is a much better place. When I first came to Old Town in 1913, I worked as a carpenter. I got three or maybe six dollars a day, but there is not much work in the winter time, and I had to go in the woods. My job as St. Joseph's Church janitor is steady the year round, and it's not hard. I have a little garden here, and I keep hens.

Work is much easier now for a woman. They have the washer, the Frigidaire, the electric light, and water in the sink.

Yes, sir, the world has improved very much since I lived in Canada.

The Rev. Wilfred Ouellette

> *Father Ouellette is nearly six feet tall, dark, and very agreeable. He wears eye glasses and has dark wavy hair. Is about 45 years old, perhaps. His face was perfectly expressionless at first, but as he talked about the French his face lighted up with interest and enthusiasm. I certainly enjoyed the interview which furnished a decided contrast to others because of the man's poise, precise speech, and wide knowledge.*
>
> R.F.G.

I'm afraid I can't tell you who the first pastor was here. Our records go back some distance, but they don't go back that far. Sometimes people who wish to apply for pensions come here to get their birth records when they can't procure them at the city hall. John Bapst was one of the early priests here. Perhaps some of the older residents could recall the name of the first pastor. I think he was Irish.

Many of the French Canadians who came to Maine sixty or seventy years ago were unable to speak English, but they could read and write French. If any were uneducated it was not the fault of the schools—they were very good. Sometimes, however, villages or farms were so isolated that it was difficult for children to reach the schools, and that fact accounted for some illiteracy.

The farms in Maine usually ran parallel to the road, but in Canada they were laid out in long, narrow strips, perpendicular to the road or river. They arranged their farms that way so that their settlement would be more compact.* They would be

---

*Of course, the farms were arranged that way to give each *habitant* access to the river. C.S.D.

near each other and able to help one another more readily. The houses were near the road, vegetables and grain for home use were planted between the house and the wood, and out in the back was the woods where they obtained their firewood. That arrangement of farms may have been influenced by the dangers of attack from hostile Indians or wild animals, but chiefly, I think, it was promoted by a desire for companionship.

There is much in this outline that you will find fully treated in this book by Bracq. You do not speak or understand French? Ah, that is too bad. Bracq lived among the people, he spoke their language, and he knew their customs. He loved them. Only in that way can one write understandingly of them. The French here are unfortunately losing many of their racial characteristics. We teach French over here in St. Joseph's Parochial School, and nearly all of the students can speak the language, but many of them, especially those who attend the public schools, can't read or write it. America is the great melting pot. All races are poured into it to emerge as one.

I wish that the French would resist that melting process more than those of other nationalities. We are loyal to the country in which we claim citizenship, but we are also loyal to ourselves and our traditions. Consider the question from another point of view. Supposing that you were a member of a small group of Americans who emigrated to a foreign land and settled on foreign soil. You would see yourselves threatened with extinction so far as your racial identity was concerned. Your little group would represent a small island that was in danger of being engulfed in the sea of a different racial culture. Would you not make an effort to preserve your racial traits? I think you would.

Quebec is predominantly French—almost as much so as France itself—but we feel that what was the old province of Acadia is almost a land apart. You have read the poem *Evangeline?* The incidents related in the poem are in the main true. Acadia came under the domination of the English at the time, and ever since, that part of Canada has remained, in contrast to the Province of Quebec, the home of mixed racial groups.

The French newspapers published in Maine were never large in size. Some had only four pages, and some had eight or ten. These publishing companies were not regarded as money making concerns. The people who started them *knew that they would lose money.* They were people who obtained an income from some other source: they were lawyers, doctors, businessmen. They did it only because of their patriotism and their love for things French. They wished to help perpetuate the language and customs of the race. Here is the *Bangor News.* Its editors have their ideals, of course, but it is strictly a commercial proposition. It can be bought and sold. These French newspapers were not regarded in that light. They were *nearer to the hearts* of their owners than to their pocketbooks. Wait, I will get one for you.

Fr. Ouellette jumped up here and ran up a stairway in the hall and returned shortly with two papers.

Ah, here is one published in Montreal: *Le Devoir.* Do you know what that means? "The Duty." This contains, as you see, ten pages, and it is equal in size to the ordinary paper. It derives its income from advertisements and from subscriptions. This one is *Le Messager* of Lewiston, and it is representative of the French papers published in Maine. On the first page is an account of the President's message to Congress, an account of the opening session of the Maine Legislature, some war news from China, a dispatch from Berlin, and some general news items. On the back pages there is news of a local and personal nature. There are some advertisements, and in general there are features that might be found in any American paper. Here is the installment of a serial story, and much of this page is devoted to editorials. Ah, those editorials! Here are many advertisements of local concerns, and this is the sports page. These papers are printed entirely in French.

Trade relations between Maine and Canada—that is out of my sphere. Literature, Arts, and Theater. We are interested in all of these things, but I do not think you will find many French persons who occupy outstanding positions in those professions in Maine. Just a minute, I have a book of biographies that I will get for you.

Again Father Ouellette ran upstairs, this time to return with a book printed in French.

This book contains brief biographies of prominent French people, not only of Maine, but of New England as well.

Music. Yes, the French are distinctly musical. They have their old folk songs, too. I have a book—the first of a series that will be published—that contains many of the old folk songs of Canada. I will get it for you.

This time the priest went out to a music room on the same floor and returned with the book mentioned.

This book was sent to me by the author whose name and picture appears on this page. The title is *Chantes La Bonne Chanson. La Feuille d'Erable*—the maple leaf is the emblem of Canada. *Evangeline, Les Cloches du Hameau*—that is very pretty. Here is a picture of the bridge at Quebec. *La Soupe aux Pois*. Of course you know the meaning of that. It means pea soup. That was almost a national dish. Many of these songs are Canadian, but some are of France. *Pot Pourri:* that means a little of everything. *Les Crêpes*. Ah, you can tell what that means by the picture. Pancakes. That dish, too, is very well liked. You must remember to write something about maple sugar. The making of that is an important industry in Canada. You may take both of these books if you wish—as the newspapers. I won't need them for a time. You may keep them as long as you require them.

Cuisine. Yes, that should be taken up. Cooking is an art in France and the French Canadians originally came from that country. Many of the French in Canada were, of course, very poor and couldn't afford choice dishes. They ate plain food, well cooked. I can't think of any dish that became so identified with the French people in Canada as pea soup. They liked meat pies.

Religion, Divorce. Divorce was unknown to these people. The people were urged to remain true to one mate. Sometimes there was a separation, but no divorce. Holiday celebrations. Christmas and New Year's were their main holidays. Epiphany, which is tomorrow (January 6), was also observed. Much of this you will find treated in Bracq's book.

Superstition. Now there is something that will have to be handled very carefully. The French are sensitive, and they would resent anything that would seem to ridicule their beliefs. Yes, it is necessary to be careful there. They had their stories and tales of ghosts and witches, but they were told with the tongue in the cheek. Someone might take a pack of cards and tell fortunes with them, but it was only for amusement. We had a fortune teller's booth at one of our entertainments a few years ago. She told fortunes with the cards, but nobody took it seriously.

It was necessary to bring the interview to a close soon after this because the duties of the priest required that he should be in the church at 3:30, and it was nearly that when I left.

Alex Lavoie

Alex Lavoie had professed an interest in the work I was doing, when I met him in Leblanc's store. Lavoie knows a lot about the old French customs and enjoys talking about them. He is about 47 years old and just now is working on a WPA road project. Leblanc is a French Canadian who came to Old Town in 1908, and he is about the same age as Lavoie. Both of them worked for a long time in the woolen mill—Lavoie as a spinner and Leblanc as a weaver. They probably would be there now if the mill had not closed. I've worked with Lavoie—or Leavitt—in the woods, on the boom, in the woolen mill, and on a road project. He is a very good worker but slow acting. Gene Mann, the boss on the boom, used to say when he saw Alex strolling down to work in the morning at the end of a long line, "Well, they must all be out of the bunk house—here is Alex." He married an American girl who was converted to the Catholic faith. The couple have two children. I had mentioned to him that Father Ouellette, whom I

> had just interviewed, couldn't tell me the name of the first pastor of St. Joseph's, in Old Town.
>
> R.F.G.

I can tell you that. It was Father Nicoli.

How did you know that?

My grandmother told me. It would be hard to prove it, I suppose, if they had no records of that time at the church, but go down to the cemetery and you'll find graves there of the three priests who died while they were in charge of this parish. The graves are all in the church lot—Father Lavadier, Father Trudel, and Father Nicoli. Nicoli was buried in another lot, but the coffin was transferred. You'll find his name on one of the monuments.

Father Ouellette said that Bapst was here before Trudel.

He was, and he was here before Nicoli, but Bapst wasn't a resident priest and Nicoli was. Bapst went from one town to another on a kind of route. Nicoli died about the year Father Trudel came here—1880.

It's too bad old Zeb, my uncle, isn't alive. He knew a lot about magic, ghosts, and superstitions. I remember a story they used to tell about a time when there was an epidemic of black cholera over on French Island. There was an old covered wooden bridge that ran across the river at that time, and guards had been stationed at this end of the bridge to prevent anyone from crossing in either direction. The Maine Central Railroad bridge wasn't there then so the only way to get to the island—unless you had a boat—was to cross by the wooden bridge.

In some way the priest got over there, but the guards said he hadn't gone across the bridge. He gave dying people extreme unction—the last sacraments, you know. He worked there until the danger was past, and then he appeared on this side again. The guards said they didn't see him cross the bridge in either direction. The old people said he walked across the water to get back and forth, but, of course, nobody would believe such a yarn as that now.

If you have to write anything about the schools, be sure to say something about that time Fatty Cyr went to night school. It was about ten years ago and they were having night school over in the French Island school. Fatty was on the police force then. It had been going along for a couple of months, and the teacher decided to find out how much they knew or had learned. She wrote some names and things on the black board.

"What's this word, Mr. Cote?" she says pointing to the first word.

"That's my name—Cote."

"Correct. Mr. Moreau, what is this word?"

"M-o-r-e-a-u. That's my name, Moreau." "Right."

"Mr. Cyr," pointing to the word *cat*. "Tell me what this is."

Fatty looked at the word for about a minute. "I suppose it's my name," he said finally, "but I can't seem to make it out."

William Green

William Green lived in Canada when young, but was born in Van Buren in 1863. 75 years old. Lives with his wife and married son, Adam, who is their only child.

Mr. Green came to Old Town to live 48 years ago in 1890, but he had been here before at different times to work. He worked in the Portsmouth Navy Yard at Portsmouth, N.H. for a year just before he came to Old Town to stay. He went to school in Van Buren about six years when he was a child. Can read and write in both French and English. He had a pronounced accent when he first came to Old Town, but that has entirely disappeared. He could speak English when he came here. He used to work a lot here as a brick and stone mason. His boy, Adam,

> *worked with him. Is a good Catholic. Mr. Green is about 5 ft. 10 inches tall, slightly stooped, tanned, white hair. His mind is quite clear, but he seems to be growing weak. He used to talk so that anyone could hear him half a block away. His son Adam does odd jobs. Worked on the WPA last winter. Adam used to work as a painter in the E.M. White canoe shop. Three of the canoes he painted while there were displayed in the window of a local drug store about 20 years ago. The coloring scheme was very unusual and original. The design on one showed life size dragon flies, on another the design was drifted autumn leaves in natural colors. I thought of the other design yesterday, but it has slipped my mind for the time. On the bow of each canoe the pattern was utilized to form the artist's name. The name didn't show up plainly, but it blended into the design. The canoes excited much favorable comment.*
>
> R.F.G.

Well, I'm afraid there isn't much that I can tell you. I wasn't born in Canada, you know. In Van Buren in 1863. We lived in Canada for a while, though.

Yes, work was hard to get up there, then, and they didn't pay anything. The pay wasn't so awful good here, but anyone could get by on it, and there was always a job. I could speak English before I came here. I worked in the woods, in the woolen mill, and in the sawmills. I did a lot of mason work, too, on sidewalks, buildings, and foundations. I worked on St. Joseph's Church when they were building that. I was out in Portsmouth, New Hampshire a couple of years in the shipyard. I used to get $1.25 a day in the sawmill, and we worked twelve hours a day. We lived over on French Island when we first came here. We had a big space for a garden then, so you can see there was a lot less people lived there then.

I asked Mr. Green about a Frank Wedge who lived across the street.

Frank? Oh yes. He's a French Canadian. He's a foreman down at the pulp mill. Works outside all the time. Has a small crew of men under him. They go around doing carpenter and repair work for the mill. He built that new carrier they have there. Pretty smart for a fellow seventy-eight years old. He doesn't get through until four o'clock.

I remarked that the name Wedge didn't sound French.

That is the English of it. In French it would be Aucoin. Yes, Green wouldn't be called a French name, either. In French it would be *Grenier*. I always had to explain how that was spelled, so I started to use the English way of it. The lawyer up there couldn't spell it.

The Whitmore and Morse Granite Quarry in East Barre, Vermont, September 1941.

Barre, Vermont

"[R]ising above it towered The Hill, its huge bulk pitted with quarries. At a distance the deep, open wounds lost their dimensions: They appeared to be gigantic scars. . . . The Hill was Granitetown's very lifeblood. It was not as beautiful as its storied sister hills of Vermont. It reared gaunt and despoiled, its rock-ribbed sides shattered and lacerated. The Hill dominated Granitetown, yet it stood there defenseless against the many and deeper wounds man would inflict in years to come. For, as long as this beautiful stone was available, there would be men to work it. . . To hew it. To carve it. To ship it to the four corners of the country, and beyond, where it would pile into lasting buildings, or stand as memorials to fellow men who had paid their visit to the world and departed." That picture of Barre, Vermont, from a novel by Federal Writers' Project interviewer Mari Tomasi, describes a setting for Franco-Americans altogether different from the textile mills of Manchester or the log booms and paper mills of Old Town.

Granite quarrying and the manufacture of granite products made Barre and brought Franco-Americans to it. Although "The Hill" had given up millstones, granite posts, and occasional door sills and foundation stones from early in the nineteenth century, the arrival of the railroad to Barre in the 1870s, created the city. Before the end of the century, "the Barre belt" of villages had become the largest granite producing region in the nation. In 1880 Barre had eight quarries and six cutting sheds. By 1895, it had 70 quarries and 300 cutting sheds. By the 1930s, the time of these life-history narratives, Barre annually shipped over 130,000 tons of granite in the rough and had a population of 11,000.

The granite industry produced a unique ethnic mix in Barre. Scottish quarrymen came from Aberdeen in the 1880s. Italian stonecutters arrived from Lombardy and Tuscany by the 1890s. Others came from Scandinavia, Ireland, and Saragossa in Spain. Later came the Franco-Americans. The ethnic mix was almost epitomized by Barre's splendid statue of Robert Burns, funded by Scots and carved by Italians.

Since most of these immigrants came from working-class rather than peasant backgrounds, they brought left-wing European ideologies with them. To be sure, a Catholic parish was organized in 1889, but as late as the 1920s its priest was Irish, and his views had a lot of competition. For example, half the city's population was Italian by World War I, but its loyalties were more likely to be Garibaldian, socialist, and anarcho-syndicalist than Catholic. By that time Barre also had a Socialist Hall, emblazoned with the arm and hammer of the Socialist Labor Party. Among its other activities, the hall housed a cooperative grocery store until 1926.

The individual ethnic organizations frequently reflected a similar left-wing orientation. From the 1890s, Barre was also a stronghold of the Quarry Workers and Granite Cutters unions. In 1912, Barre granite worker families took in over 50 children from strike-torn Lawrence, Massachusetts. The publicity surrounding these evacuated children won public support for that historic strike. On several occasions, socialist union leaders won mayoralty elections on "citizen's" tickets. Old-timers could remember hearing political speakers as varied as Emma Goldman, Bill Haywood, Eugene Debs, and, during the Spanish Civil War, Urribe and a female lieutenant of "La Pasionaria." Workers contributed enough money to buy an ambulance for Loyalist Spain. In the depression year of 1937, with probably fewer than 1000 members, the Barre locals of the Granite Cutters International Association raised $3000, a sizeable figure in those days, to help striking Elberton, Georgia granite cutters win a union shop. This continuing left-wing activity testifies to a kind of politics unexpected in one of only two states to vote for Republican Alf Landon for president in 1936.

One other continuing phenomenon shaped Barre in those years. That was the high incidence of stonecutters' tuberculosis, silicosis. "And they would come over here, these immigrants," recalled one of them in the 1960s, "rosy cheeks, healthy, young, and in a few years, they were dead—and we didn't know what was killing them." In 1919, a local physician, D.C. Jarvis, concluded that the cause was granite dust. A 1923-1925 U.S. Public Health Service study confirmed his conclusion. In 1928, the Harvard School of Public Health began research on devices to reduce the amount of dust in the quarries and manufacturing sheds.

These studies demonstrated that the rising rate of silicosis resulted from the introduction of pneumatic tools in the 1890s and their general use after 1900. Although the percentage of Vermont deaths from tuberculosis fell from 9.1% in 1900 to 6.7% in 1931, the rate among granite workers rose dramatically in the same period. Fifty percent died of silicosis in 1900; 75% did so in 1931. Vermont's tuberculosis death rate was New England's highest, and 45% of Vermont's tuberculosis deaths occurred in the county surrounding Barre.

A solution to silicosis came only in the late 1930s, not from government initiatives or the good-will of employers, but from collective bargaining agreements won by unions to require suction devices on all pneumatic tools. Until then the only palliatives were the TB sanitorium on Barre's outskirts and the benefit dances held in Socialist Hall for victims. The spectre of silicosis stalked Barre's workers, their widows, and their orphans, as the Federal Writers' Project life-history narratives will show. In her novel about Barre, Mari Tomasi could have one of her characters only mildly amused by the double entendre of a song sung to the tune of *You're in the Army Now:*

> You're diggin' a tombstone now,
> You might as well take your bow,
> This old stone hole
> Will take its toll,
> You're diggin' a tombstone now.

While silicosis cast a permanent shadow over Barre's working families, the strike of 1922 was the traumatic single event in their memories, if we are to believe these life-history narratives. Barre's unionized workers had won good wages and a forty-hour week by the end of World War I. Right after the war, hard times and anti-union sentiment caused Barre manufacturers, like their fellow managers at Amoskeag, to cut wages and attack the unions. At the end of 1921, granite cutters refused a wage cut to $6.40 a day, and a strike and lock-out gripped Barre through 1922. Three-fourths of Barre's workers were involved. To break the strike, quarry and shed owners brought in hundreds of French Canadian strikebreakers from Quebec farms, surrounded them with police protection, and defeated the unions. By 1923, the unions were able to maintain themselves in a few firms at $8.00 a day wages, but most Barre firms adopted the open shop and the 1921 wage offer. The rise in the number of Franco-American parishioners from 522 in 1922 to 1150 in 1925 reflected the arrival of these French strikebreakers, but the parish census says nothing of the certain rifts in the working class neighborhoods in the 1920s between the majority of non-unionized workers and the minority of unionized ones.

Difficulties continued as management tried to cope with the Great Depression through ruinous price and wage cutting. The granite cutters union accepted a 1932 wage cut to $6.00 a day. That alarmed non-union men, who could expect only $4.00 a day for themselves, so that they joined with the union in a new strike in April, 1933. The evidence is fragmentary, but it appears that this time, Franco-American workers had become unionists. For example, the union local of polishers and another of tool sharpeners were headed by French-surnamed leaders. An Italian American organizer with "a lot of friends amongst the French Canadians" claimed that he "organized more French Canadians in the union that any several people in the town." Three thousand workers shut down all but one of Barre's sheds. Sheriff's deputies and militia circulated through town; heads were occasionally bashed; strikers were jailed. Finally arbitration brought a settlement which anticipated the National Recovery Act formula of the following year. A 1937 agreement postponed wage increases in favor of the adoption of suction devices for each machine to reduce the dust which caused silicosis. By 1939, the sheds were 75% unionized, and even polishers received wage raises to $8.25 a day. It would take a few more years to unionize the quarry workers.

An overview such as this cannot capture the impact of these developments on individual lives. For example, what does it mean, in a city of 11,000, for 165 granite cutters to die of silicosis between 1931 and 1935? Or, what does it mean for families when, according to a union official in 1934, only 275 cutters were working, 400-450 were unemployed with 200-300 of these being unemployed for two or three years? Answers to questions like these can better come from reading the following life-history narratives of individual Franco-Americans in Barre. All of them were written down by Mari Tomasi, the Federal Writers' Project interviewer.

SOURCES

Barre in Retrospect, 1776-1976 (Barre: Friends of the Aldrich Public Library, 1975).

Roby Colodny, "Labor in Barre: 1900-1941" in Robert Mueller, *et al.*, *Vermont's Untold Story* (Burlington: Frayed Page Collective, 1976), pp. 14-17.

Granite Cutters Journal, 1931-1939.

Guide Franco-American (Fall River: 1922-1946).

Bernard Sanders (ed.), "Vermont Labor Agitator," *Labor History*, 15 (1974), 261-270. Interview with Mose Gerasoli.

Mari Tomasi, *Like Lesser Gods* (Milwaukee, 1949).

Stonecutter

Rae was short and stocky. A reddish brown moustache almost covered his short upper lip; above that his wide rather flat nose was red, too. The painful red of sunburn from outdoor work.

"I take whatever work I can get," he said. "Right now it's WPA. Digging ditches. It's better than nothing. I haven't a family, so I manage to get along with the little I earn.

"I can cut stone. I've done it on and off for thirteen years. I can't say I like it. The pay is good, but whenever I get a chance for another work I grab it. I've seen too many of these stonecutters' lives shortened. I don't want it to happen to me. I went into the sheds in the first place because I couldn't find other work. I still work there once in a while.

"I came here from Canada when I was around fifteen. My mother, sister and I had been living there while my father worked in the Barre sheds. I had one year of high school here in Barre, then I found work helping a bricklayer. It didn't pay much because I just helped a few hours a day. My father had been working in the sheds all his life; he died two years after I quit school. The only reason I went into the sheds then was because I needed more money to support myself and my mother. She was always after me to quit the sheds; I didn't like it anyways so whenever any other job showed up I grabbed it.

"Yes, my father was working here before the big strike. I remember him saying he was ashamed of those French who came in to put a stop to the strike. Some of them couldn't be blamed, he said, they didn't know what it was all about. They couldn't appreciate the dangers of stonecutting. Some of them had never seen a shed before. They couldn't understand that these cutters had a right to strike, and that they deserved as much pay as they could get. Many of these strikebreakers left Barre afterwards; they were cold-shouldered and looked down upon; they couldn't stand it. The ones that stuck to the sheds and are still working feel different about it now. I'll bet you couldn't get one of them to go now to some other granite area as a strikebreaker, not for twice the money they're earning. Lots of them are still ashamed of what they did. They don't even want to speak about it; that's why it's difficult for you to get much information from these French. With some of them it was a hard lesson. They learned that from the snubs and the cold looks they got from the people they had to meet and mingle with every day.

"If I had a chance to go in the sheds now, I suppose I would take it—it would mean more money—and leave this job for someone who isn't trained to do other work.

"I'm not married. I room on Maple Street. There are four roomers at the house; one of them is a stonecutter. Yes, he's

French. I don't know when he came here, but he's been working in the sheds as long as I've known him which is about ten years. He tells me he was engaged to be married once, and they had the date set and all. But one day she up and told him that if he didn't find some other work outside of a shed she wouldn't marry him. Her own people had been in the granite business, and she said she wanted to break away from it. She'd already seen too much worry and sickness. Well, this Al, that's his name, didn't know any other trade; besides he was peeved, said it was a devil of a time to tell him when the date was set and all, so it ended right there. They never got married, he tells me, and this is the funny part of it: she was married a couple of years later and to a stonecutter.

"I've lived in several rooming houses. Most of the landladies were wives of Italian or French granite workers. Most of them had good-sized families, too. I've noticed that in the French houses the children are made to speak the native language more than in the Italian homes. I lived with some Italian people for a year; the man was my shed boss. The two oldest children spoke Italian fairly well; the three younger ones could understand it, but I never heard them speak it. I don't know why it is, but the French seem more eager to keep their language alive."

Boardinghouse Keeper

Woodbine shaded most of the kitchen porch. Where the sun lay in patches on the floor, leaf-shaped patterns moved silently back and forth. The French woman sat in a rocker, peeling potatoes. A pail, standing on a stool in front of her, received the peels; she dropped the potatoes in a white-enameled pan at her right.

"You will excuse me if I go right on and peel," Mrs. Lachance said. "I have just so much time before supper, and there are so many things to be done. Potatoes! It seems I must cook mountains of them to satisfy the men. Ten of them here, and all but one are stonecutters."

She was a middle-aged woman, plump, red-cheeked, pleasant. "I have had as many as eighteen boarding here, but with that number I have to take on an extra girl. With only ten, my daughter and myself manage. If my daughter happens to want the evening, we hire a girl from next door to help with the dishes.

"No, I have not always taken in boarders. It is only since my husband died nine years ago. Before that, I did not have to. He made enough for us to get along well. He was a letter carver. Seventeen years he'd worked at it. Most of the time in Barre, but one year in Montpelier.

"I do not take roomers, you can see the house is not big enough for that. Since two of the girls were married we have given one upstairs bedroom to the family on the other side. My youngest girl graduates from high school next year. There was an older boy, but he died at the time of the 'flu.' He was just a baby.

"I was born here in Barre. My husband came down from Chambly, Canada with his folks when he was a boy. They were a farming family. He started working in the sheds when he was eighteen. Doing odd labor, but he worked up to a letter carver. He made good money, but I was not happy having him in the sheds. It's bad, especially for a man with a family, and most of the French stonecutters around here have large families. I have a neighbor a few houses down the street who had more than her share of unhappiness from her husband's work in the sheds. He died the year after my own husband. Yes, his lungs. Since then two of his boys have died from the same thing. The remaining boy and girl are far from well. The girl has been to a preventorium for six months; the boy has to take very good care of himself. He works in an office. Sometimes I think the granite isn't worth all of the sorrow it brings, but it's there in the earth, it's worth money to the owners, and if a man works there, well, he's the fool for doing it. There's no one to blame but himself. My husband used to say so; he still said so when he was flat on his back. You'd think it would have made him bitter. It didn't. He was resigned to it. He accepted it as something he had expected all along. He didn't mind talking to me about it, but when his friends visited him—other stonecutters—neither he nor they would mention the sickness that takes so many of them. Perhaps they are all like that. Perhaps in their families they will discuss it, but not with others. I suppose it is like any deep misfortune or unhappiness; you will talk about it only to those who are dear to you—or, sometimes, to a stranger you never expect to see again."

Mrs. Lachance paused to give orders concerning the supper to her daughter who had appeared at the kitchen door. She was a small girl with her mother's red cheeks, and an abundance of black, wavy hair. Underneath the apron she wore was a black and white checked taffeta dress. When she had disappeared into the kitchen, the mother confided in a low voice, "She's going to a dance tonight at Joe's Pond. That's why she's all dressed for going out. She goes with a French boy." She hesitated as if undecided to continue. She rubbed a finger over a puckered forehead. She sighed, "Well, I guess I don't mind your knowing it. She goes with that boy I was telling you about, the one who lost his father and two brothers. He's a fine boy. I like him, but I can't help but wish that it was someone else. Someone strong and well. I'd hate to think of her losing her husband as I did. Usually they are sick for a long time, months of sorrow and heartache. And afterwards, to be left alone with your children. To struggle the best you can. Ah, yes, it is a hard life. Sometimes I have wanted to speak to her, but then I think she knows the story as well as I do. It will do no good. She will do what she wants, and it is her life to live."

The potatoes were fast piling up as Mrs. Lachance spoke. She smiled, "Almost enough. Now, my other two daughters have married well. One with a French boy from Chambly. Leota met him when she was visiting her father's people. They are living there now with her grandparents. No, my father-in-law didn't like stonecutting. They went back to the farm after a few years. The other girl is married to an Italian. He sells insurance here in Barre.

"Do I like Barre? Well, I've lived here all my life. I could have moved to Quincy when I married. My husband had an offer from a shed down there. But I was satisfied with Barre. It's just large enough, the stores are good, and there's always been lively enough excitement for the children. I don't think you could find a better high school than Spaulding in the State. The only fault I find with Barre is that there are not enough jobs in town for the young people when they get out of high school. Many of them get office jobs in Montpelier; the rest have to go to larger cities. You don't see many of the high school educated boys going into the sheds. You can't blame them. There's nothing of a future for them there, not now.

"The big strike? I don't know much about it. I used to. My husband struck along with the rest of them. I used to hear him talk about it a lot, but it was all so long ago. You hear so little about it now that I've forgotten. I *do* remember my husband saying that some of the unskilled French who came in to break the strike could be excused. That was quite a statement from my husband, he was as much against them as anybody. One of those strikebreakers was a friend of his. They'd grown up together in Chambly, good friends. He hadn't seen or heard from him for years. Then all of a sudden he sees him parading through town with the rest of them. My husband was dazed; he could hardly believe it. This friend, Pete was his name, came up to the house to see my husband the next day. He'd inquired around town and found out his address. At first I thought they were coming to blows. My husband was no mild man, and he was firm in the belief that this herd of strangers was ruining the granite industry, not only the wages and the hours, but the work itself. But then Pete explained why he had come to Barre.

"Perhaps Pete's story is the same as many of those strangers' who came into Barre. I don't know. To him this opportunity for work was a godsend. He was badly in need of money. His farm, like so many other other French farms that year, was not paying. The crops amounted to nothing at all. He had a wife and three children to feed. He could see no signs of work for him in Chambly. Not for months. Then this opportunity for work in Barre came to him. Work meant keeping his family together. Can you blame him for accepting it? I don't. He'd never worked in granite. Never touched it before. He'd heard, of course, of Barre and the granite workers. But he knew of them vaguely, just as he knew of miners and steel workers. I mean, how hard the work was, and dangerous. But he had to be amongst the workers, live with them and do their work, before he could really appreciate the fact that they needed a strike to better their conditions. No, Pete came here to Barre absolutely ignorant of the granite business and the people in it. He came for work, for money to keep his family together. You can't be too hard on him. I don't blame him. I haven't seen much of him since my husband died. But I know he's a union man now, and a good one."

Mrs. Lachance called to her daughter that the potatoes were ready. She leaned back in her chair and began to rock lazily, comfortably. "You know," she said, "the longer you live in this world the better you realize that there are always two sides to a question. And it isn't fair to judge until you know and study both sides.

"No, I wasn't thinking only of the strike. Of course, that *is* one of those two-sided questions. Right now I'm thinking of a woman who lives down the street. An Italian woman. She sells beer and wine. Hard stuff, too. She's had to pay a fine twice for selling without a license. She still sells. I don't blame her. Some of the neighbors look down on her. They don't want their children to play with hers. Her husband died a few years ago. Yes, his lungs, too. He was a stonecutter. She had six children. None of them big enough to be working. Her hip was badly crushed the year after her husband died. What was she to do? She had to find some way of feeding those children. It's hard for her to get around. There aren't many kinds of work she can do. The easiest way—so it seemed to her—was to sell liquor in her own house. That way she could be at home all the time to look after her children. Yes, it's illegal. But there's her side, too. She wants her children. She wants to keep them together. She's proud. She doesn't want charity. She does Italian baking, too. That brings in a little money."

Granite Worker

Alcide Savoie was a squat, stocky Frenchman. He sucked contentedly at a curved, worn pipe. "I've had almost twenty years of the sheds," he said, "ever since 1921. And," he added, "I've boarded and roomed in this house for ten years."

It was a characterless house, one of three similar structures set back from Berlin Street with always a view of a dismal line of sheds. The house was a three-storied wooden square, painted green. Mrs. LaCrosse, a stonecutter's widow, was the landlady.

"I came down from Iberville, Canada," Savoie went on. "I had no intention of coming to Barre or working in the sheds. I'd been out of a job for a few weeks, then I heard that cottages were going up fast at Mallett's Bay on Lake Champlain. I knew a little about carpentering. I managed to get a job there through the summer until late fall. Well, I hated to go back to Iberville. There was nothing there for me, so I started looking around. About this time the shed owners in the Barre district were complaining about the high wages they had to pay skilled workers, and it seems they were willing to break in new workers to save their pocketbooks. Good carvers were getting $20.00 or more a day, but I'll say they deserved it. Their work meant everything to them. Anyway, that's how I got my chance to go in the sheds. I can't say I'm sorry—not yet. I work hard, and I feel fine. I've worked up to *sawyer*, that means $8.50 a day, pretty good pay these days.

"My first year in Barre I roomed in a business block on North Main Street. I wasn't lonesome. There were a lot of Canadians coming in from just north of Vermont. Some of us got in the habit of having our meals out together. We'd always take in the church suppers—it was good cooking and a change from the restaurants.

"That's how I met my landlady, at a supper the St. Ann's Society was giving. The society was just for married French women. A Catholic society. Mrs. LaCrosse did the cooking that night, and we all thought is was fine. Her husband had died of stonecutter's T.B. the month before. She told us she was going to invest her insurance money in a good, plain house and take in boarders and roomers. Four of us moved in the next week. She made a pretty good living out of it. Another granite worker's widow, she was French too, rented the house next door the following year and took in boarders. The two women were friendly, but they knew we talked a lot about the food and compared meals, so there got to be plenty of competition. It suited us fine. Each one would plan the best meals she could afford and still make a profit. I'd never eaten so well before, and I haven't since. It didn't last more than a year. The French woman next door married again, another stonecutter. He said he had to work in the sheds all day; he didn't want to be looking at them at night. They moved to the other end of town.

"Most of the roomers in this house are working in the sheds or quarries. The landlady treats us as if we were her family. In September of 1938, the Commissioner of Industries of Vermont issued the regulation enforcing the use of goggles by various quarry workers, and refusing compensation unless the driller was wearing them at the time his eye was injured by either a granite or steel chip. Before this, Mrs. LaCrosse used to keep after a couple of the quarry workers and see that they had goggles. In the winter, when they carried their lunch, she made sure the glasses were packed in their boxes. Only men operating plug drills, jackhammers, lime drills, bull-sets, bit-grinders and emery wheels are requested by the Commissioner to wear them. Owners of the quarries are ordered to provide the goggles. If they fail they are subject to penalty. If an injury is received by a worker whose employer has failed to provide goggles, he may collect compensation. It's a good regulation, and most of the fellows stick to it, even though it is a bother to those who aren't used to them. Sometimes I wear them in the sheds. It's funny, if a man hurts his eye today the rest of the men are sure to wear goggles for a week or two. Then they discard them until the next accident. But we don't get as many eye injuries in the sheds as they do in the quarries."

Stonecutters, Father and Son

His long, lean face was the brown of outdoor living, and his tall body slender and sinewy. Had he smiled to lift the weary droop of his mouth and chase the disturbing resignation from his eyes, you would have said his was a rugged, happy health.

You felt instinctively that here was a sadness, a sorrow he might have hidden from your eyes a score of years back when he was 40 or 45 years old. Now his figure drooped its resignation to the world.

He sat on a rough square of granite beside a new garage watching a man hosing the car in the next yard. "He's my son," he said with a quiet pride in the fine body and wiry suppleness he had given the younger man. "He's the oldest. With his face turned from us, the way it is now, you'd almost think he was my age. There's more grey in his hair than in mine. It's the life he leads. Drinking, staying out half the night." Scorn tinged his low-spoken words. "He doesn't know how to drink. None of these young fellows do. I've seen him make a week-long celebration of it, and then spend another week getting rid of a hangover. He's lost his job twice because of that. Both times I managed to get him another. I'm well known in the sheds in Barre and Montpelier; I've lived here ever since I was sixteen. My folks came down from Quebec. I learned the trade those first years in Vermont, and I've been working in the sheds ever since. I've a daughter who's married and settled in Taunton, Massachusetts and a younger boy who graduates from high school this year. I'll see to it that this boy doesn't go into the sheds. I used to say that about the oldest one, too, but he got into them just the same. After he quit school he lazed around for a whole year. I don't believe he worked more than three weeks out of fifty-two. I told him he ought to be ashamed of himself when he had such a fine, strong body. Well, he got a chance then to go in the sheds, and though I hated to see him doing that work, I knew it would be better than loafing. It would make a working man out of him. He's still lazy. There are plenty of times during the year when the sheds close down from lack of work, so many times that a good worker complains. But not my boy. He takes extra days off besides. Whenever he wants to. We used to have arguments over it, but I've kept quiet the last few years. He's old enough now to know how he wants to live. I guess he'll never marry, he'll have to change his way of living if he does. Maybe he's wise in having a good time. I don't know. I've seen a lot of these stonecutters in my life. Maybe these younger ones are wise to cram their good times and wild times in a short space of years.

"I'll tell you something now that won't sound pleasant to you. I'm sick. My lungs. I kept working as long as I could. The doctor made me quit three weeks ago. He wanted me to go to a sanatorium then, but I wanted to see my youngest boy graduate. I was afraid if I went there they wouldn't let me out for the day. He graduates next week. The following week I suppose I will have to go. Yes, I could stay home since we have no small children, but it would be too much of a strain on my wife. She's nervous and excitable. Besides the doctor says it will be better for me there. I've been thinking of it lots at night, when everyone is asleep. I've been thinking how nice it would be to stay here at home without working for the whole summer. It's funny sometimes how little things will please you, little things you can have by raising your finger, and still you deny yourself the pleasure they might bring. Perhaps it's because down inside of you you know that in bringing you happiness it may be doing harm to those you care for. I guess that's why I've decided it's for the best after all to go to the sanatorium. A friend of mine up the street, he was a stonecutter years ago, went to California last year when he was told his lungs were bad. He's back home now abed. I say it's a waste of money. It may drag your life out for a few months more, but what good does it do anyone? You're spending money that your family could well use after you're gone.

"Yes, there are a great many French in the granite industry, both in the sheds and in the quarries. I'd say they were here before the Italians and Scotch. They heard of these 'granite mines' as they called them, and they came down off their Canadian farms to find work. But, of course, the skilled ones were chiefly Italian and Scotch who'd learned the trade in their own country. It's pretty hard to pass judgment on the French who came in the '20s. Yes, they were certainly strikebreakers, but there are two sides to the question. Most of them were men who had to have work; it was a job to them. If the union men wanted to keep them out of the industry, why did they teach these newcomers the trade? That's what they did. These French made money for the shed owners, they put out a lot of memorials, but they were plain work and of little beauty.

The owners will admit today that that period was a thorn in the granite industry.

"I work in the Barre sheds, but I live in Montpelier. We moved here from Barre five years ago. We're Catholics, and my wife wanted the youngest boy to go to a Catholic high school. There was just the Catholic grade school in Barre. Well, it was a choice of the boy's driving to Montpelier to school, or my driving to Barre to work. I decided I might as well be the one to get the early morning air. We didn't own the house in Barre so it made it simpler moving down here. No, we haven't made any plans for moving back now that the boy is graduating. My wife likes Montpelier, she likes her neighbors, and now that I'll be going to the hospital, having friends around her will be nice for her."

Woonsocket, Rhode Island

Like Manchester, Woonsocket was a textile city. Born of that same industrial revolution in textiles which created Manchester, Woonsocket had a different development: it produced mainly woolens, not cotton; its many factories remained independent from one another rather than coming together into a Woonsocket version of the Amoskeag; and its Franco-American population was much denser than that of Manchester. Woonsocket's population was less than half that of Manchester, but its Franco-American population constituted over 70% of the city's 49,000 people in 1930. No wonder Woonsocket was called *la ville la plus française aux Etats-Unis*. These factors made its Franco-American life considerably different from that of Manchester.

At Woonsocket the Blackstone River drops 39 feet in less than a mile. In the 1830s that water power was canalized and textile factories begun. After the Civil War, woolen textile manufacturing increased until its production became more important than that of cotton textiles by 1900. In the twenty years after 1890, American-owned woolen firms were joined by several Belgian and French-owned firms which introduced the "French System" of manufacture. Under the "French System" spinning was done by European-built mules rather than by the more common cap and ring spinners. The system also required the importation of French and Belgian mule spinners.

Most cotton mills had moved South by the time of the Federal Writers' Project interviews, leaving Woonsocket with forty-five woolen mills, owned by thirty-three local and absentee companies. Most of the mills were small. Only six of them employed over 500 workers each. In addition, Woonsocket had a small machine tool industry and a rubber company. This economic development meant that Woonsocket evolved differently from Manchester. Instead of being a one-company, one-factory city, management and labor were dispersed among many companies, factories, and industries. Moreover, unlike those New England cities such as Manchester whose economies were based on declining cotton textiles, Woonsocket's woolen industry maintained the city's prosperity until the Great Depression.

The Franco-American experience in Woonsocket superficially resembled but was markedly different from that of Manchester. Of course, as for Manchester, post-Civil War Quebec families, principally from the Richelieu Valley, came to Woonsocket through "chain migration" to find work in the textile mills through "chain employment." Woonsocket's Franco-American population rose from 794 in 1860 to 5,953 in 1880 to 17,000 in 1900—60 percent of the city's total population. It would later rise to 70 percent. As in Manchester, the establishment of French parish churches verified this rising population—Precieux-Sang in 1876, Ste. Anne in 1890, Sainte Famille and St. Louis in 1902, Notre Dame des Victoires in 1909 and St. Joseph in 1929. They were accompanied by an orphanage and an old people's home, a French-language daily newspaper, and the headquarters of a fraternal insurance company, the 40,000 member Union St. Jean-Baptiste d'Amérique.

Three quarters of Franco-American children attended parochial elementary and secondary schools where French was a language of instruction. The *Guide Franco-Americain* would proudly claim eighteen French, Belgian, or Franco-American owned Woonsocket industries, over half the total, in great contrast to the Amoskeag's domination of Manchester. Such owners, coupled with the usual array of Franco-American lawyers, doctors, politicians, and merchants constituted a Franco-American elite unique to New England in power and influence. Little wonder then, that the Federal Writers' Proj-

WOONSOCKET, RHODE ISLAND 121

Two views of Woonsocket, Rhode Island, in December 1940.

ect guide to Rhode Island could claim that in Woonsocket "French is the prevailing tongue. It is heard in the streets, shops, mills, and parks. There are French newspapers, French 'talkies' in the theaters, and French radio programs. Americanisms are often admitted, so that at a baseball game one may sometimes hear such expressions as, 'Frappe un home-run, Joe!' or 'Attende un base on balls!' In general, however, the speech of the French has been remarkably persistent."

Two other developments, however, separated the Woonsocket Franco-American experience from that of Manchester or other New England cities. One was the French struggle against "Americanization" in the 1920s. In 1922, in response to a nation-wide rising tide of hostility to foreign-born Americans, the Rhode Island legislature passed the Peck Act, later declared unconstitutional, requiring English as the language of instruction in parochial schools in all subjects except religion and language. In the same year the Irish American bishop of Providence, Woonsocket's diocese, launched a fund-raising drive to build a bilingual high school in Woonsocket under diocesan, not local, control. Each French parish was given a three-year fund-raising quota. Convinced that these two events were connected, Woonsocket's Franco-American elite initially rallied the city's Franco-American working class to oppose the Irish bishop's threat to language maintenance and parish control of school finance. By 1926, with the failure of petitions to both bishop and pope in order to reverse the high school's orientation, one faction of Woonsocket's elite became more militant. It operated a newspaper, *La Sentinelle*, and conducted mass rallies in the open air to mobilize support for a boycott of the bishop's fund drive. It even appealed to the civil courts. In turn, the bishop excommunicated the *Sentinelliste* leadership, suspended *Sentinelliste* priests, and prevented *Sentinellistes* from attending church services. By 1929, the *Sentinellistes* had surrendered. Yet, the controversy split the Franco-American community, dividing elite members from each other. More important in the long run, however, it divided the Franco-American working class from its elite leadership.

A second development among the Franco-Americans of Woonsocket made their experience unique. In the 1930s, that same community which had been dominated by the bitter and ultra-conservative *Sentinelliste* controversy formed itself into one of the most radical and inclusive trade union movements in the nation. Possibly those seemingly opposite movements were connected. Some modest union organizing had occurred in cotton textiles prior to *Sentinellisme*. In 1927, just before the height of the *Sentinelliste* agitation, Woonsocket's two largest cotton textile mills closed down when their 1200 workers refused to go from a 48 to a 54 hour week. Perhaps it was coincidence that those mills lay in the neighborhoods where *Sentinelliste* rallies had their largest attendance. Or, perhaps the unemployed workers perceived those rallies as a way to protest both bishop and boss. If so, the defeat of the *Sentinelliste* leadership in 1929 prevented it from mobilizing the far greater social discontent of the Great Depression. Between 1930 and 1934 Woonsocket lost 3000 more jobs, an extremely large number considering the city had a work force of only 13,000.

With the economic downturn deepening and with the traditional Franco-American leadership split and discredited by *Sentinellisme*, Woonsocket's Franco-Americans turned to new leadership with the founding of the Independent Textile Union in 1931. By 1939, the I.T.U. had enrolled 10,000 members, 90% of Woonsocket's textile work force. The original leaders were not Franco-Americans. Rather, they were members of Woonsocket's 1500-member Franco-Belgian community, brought over by French mill owners from such socialist and anarcho-syndicalist textile centers as Roubaix-Tourcoing and Verviers. The Franco-Belgian leaders won over their Franco-American fellow workers by speaking in French, by downplaying their anticlericalism, and by concentrating on anarcho-syndicalism's appeal for community-controlled trade unionism. Surely these new leaders, so foreign to the Franco-American experience, could not have succeeded except for the discrediting and fragmenting of the old leaders by the defeat of *Sentinellisme*. By the end of the 1930s the I.T.U.'s success in organizing and its victorious strikes allowed it to humanize the workplace, control Woonsocket politics, and engage in an elaborate social and cultural program. The union's leadership fought off a strong Church counterattack through a campaign of Americanism, successfully convincing its Franco-American membership to learn English and to use American democracy and citizenship to improve its lot. Although the I.T.U. leadership had fallen to Franco-Americans and had accommodated itself to the Church by the end of World War II, Woonsocket's Franco-American workers had become organized earlier and more completely than anywhere else in New England.

The only life-history narrative to come from Woonsocket ignores these two developments, *Sentinellisme* and the Independent Textile Union. The narrator, Henry Boucher, evidently found other events more important to his experience. Born on Social Street of parents from the lower Richelieu Valley, Boucher grew up in poverty, attended Francophone parochial schools and barely learned English. At age fourteen, having passed a test on his scholastic ability by merely writing his name and address, he left school for work in the mill, where a brother already worked. In the mills Boucher "found that it would be impossible for any girl or boy, working there, to remain innocent of the facts of life, as sex was almost the only topic of conversation in the spinning room."

He accomplished other rites of passage into manhood—frequenting the saloon, chewing tobacco, and buying silk shirts and a Ford car. After a "wild party with everyone drinking, telling stories and singing the French songs of Old Canada," he went off to fight in World War I. After the war he finally ceased to be a rebel, married a *Canadienne* after a stag party which featured a strip teaser from Boston. His account of the 1920s is not that of *Sentinellisme* or the closing of cotton textile mills, but of prospering and raising a family. Fortunately for him and his family, he worked in woolen textiles. Those good years ended in 1931 when, as he says, "the bottom dropped out of everything." For him the 1930s were not years of union organizing, but of selling his possessions to provide food, clothing, rent, and coal for his family, of bread lines and soup kitchens, and of occasional employment under the changed working conditions of the "speed-up" alternated with "the ordeal of informing my wife and children that I had been laid off" and would have to go on relief.

In Henry Boucher's narrative, however, there still may be certain connections to those more dramatic events of the 1920s and 1930s. His accounts of the shop floor, one of the best in existence, demonstrate that an initiation of hazing inducted one into a tightly-knit community of work, a community which preceded and perhaps facilitated unionization. Though a member of the Social District, Woonsocket's tightest Franco-American neighborhood, he was close enough to Franco-Belgian workers, possibly some of the same ones who led the union organizing drive of the 1930s, to be given French names and addresses when he went off to World War I. Except for "the songs of Old Canada," Boucher shows scarcely any Franco-American identity. Perhaps that is because the interviewer, not a Franco-American, left it out. Or, perhaps by the time of the interview Boucher had come to view his past through the secularism and Americanism of the I.T.U. His experience and friendships in the workplace might have secularized him early in life, in contrast to the average Woonsocket Franco-American experience. Or, it might be that the experience and aspirations of Boucher, growing up in the new twentieth century, were typical of his second-generation Franco-American contemporaries.

SOURCES

Pierre Anctil, "Aspects of Class Ideology in a New England Ethnic Minority: The Franco-Americans of Woonsocket, Rhode Island (1865-1929)," Ph.D. Dissertation, New School for Social Research, 1979.

Gary Gerstle, "The Rise of Industrial Unionism: Class, Ethnicity and Labor Organization in Woonsocket, Rhode Island, 1931-1941," Ph.D. Dissertation, Harvard University, 1982. For a short account, see his "The Mobilization of the Working Class Community: The Independent Textile Union in Woonsocket, 1931-1946," *Radical History Review*, 17 (Spring, 1978), 161-172.

Richard S. Sorrell, "The Sentinelle Affair (1924-1929) and Militant *Survivance:* The Franco-American Experience in Woonsocket, Rhode Island," Ph.D. Dissertation, State University of New York at Buffalo, 1975. For a short account, see his "Sentinelle Affair (1924-1929)-Religion and Militant *Survivance* in Woonsocket, Rhode Island," *Rhode Island History*, 36 (August, 1977), 67-79.

Henry Boucher, Textile Worker

I was born in a basement on Social Street, March 27, 1898. My parents, Henry and Marie Boucher, had emigrated from the village of St. Ours, Quebec to Woonsocket in 1870. I had four brothers and two sisters, all of whom were born in Woonsocket, and I was the youngest member of the family. Due to an illness my mother was unable to work in the mill, and the small pay that my father made did not permit our having any luxuries. During slack times in the mills we were often without many of the necessities of life.

My father, an honest, hardworking cotton mill hand who had very little education, scarcely able to read and write, was always willing to work. After finishing his day's work in the mill he would saw cord wood into stove lengths for anyone who would employ him. For this he received one dollar a cord. We were very poor, and my first recollection is of the pot of pea soup that was always simmering on the stove. This pea soup and a few slices of bread, covered with lard, formed our regular diet when work was slack. Why, I was working before I had my first taste of butter.

As soon as I was able to walk I would help my older brothers as they scoured the nearby woods for firewood, and with bags we would walk along the railroad tracks looking for coal that had dropped from the coal cars. At the age of seven I entered the Jesus and Marie Convent. After spending four years in this school I was promoted to the Precious Blood College. Both of these were French parochial schools. The Precious Blood College was a grammar school, and here I was taught to read and write in French. One hour a day the English language was taught in this school, but as only French was spoken both in my house and in the Social District where I lived, I was unable to speak the English language fluently.

The one bright spot in my life at this time was the spring when my Uncle Hector, a woodchopper who lived with us during the summer, arrived in Woonsocket after working all winter in the woods of Maine. He always brought presents to us children, and we eagerly awaited his arrival. Leaving the big woods with a loaf of bread and a gallon of whiskey, so that he would not starve during the long train ride, he would land in Woonsocket, march up to our house and shout, "Hey, Marie! I've come back for a visit. What have you got to drink?" My mother would answer, "Water is the best thing for you." Hector would burst into laughter and say, "Water is only good for carrying logs, not for drinking. I am going to get something to drink." So saying he would walk off in search of the nearest saloon. If he found any other woodchoppers in the saloon, we might not see him for two days. Although he drank enough whiskey to kill two ordinary men, I never saw him unable to walk straight. While at our house he would pay five dollars a week for board and room, and he was always willing to tell us children stories of the big woods. At the close of summer he would leave Woonsocket and return to Maine.

In 1912 at the age of fourteen I left school, and presenting my birth certificate to the Superintendent of Schools, asked for permission to go to work. He told me that I would have to pass a test as to my scholastic ability. Calling me into another room, he handed me a sheet of paper and a pencil and said, "Write your name and address near the top of that paper." This I did, and apparently that was the test, for after he glanced at the paper he made out my working papers without saying a word.

My older brother found a job for me in the card room of the Lippitt mill. My task was to keep the automatic feed of four cards full of wool. For this work I received seven dollars a week. We worked 55 hours a week then. About an hour after I started working a man who was changing the gears on my card turned to me and said, "Say, kid, run down to the machine shop and get me a left-handed monkey wrench. I broke the one I had. Now make sure you bring back a left-handed wrench." This was my first errand, and I was determined to do it quickly so I ran all the way to the machine shop. Stepping up to a machinist I said, "Pete, the card fixer, wants a left-handed monkey wrench." He looked at me and said, "So you're after that wrench, are you? Hell, I don't know where it went. Ask that fellow over there—he might have it." I went over to that man and repeated my request. Although he did not have the wrench he knew where it was, so he said, "Go up to the spinning room, and ask Joe for the wrench. He has it." Running up to the spinning room, I found Joe and asked him for the wrench. He told me that he had just let a man from the weave room take it. In this manner I chased all over the mill until I arrived in my brother's room. When I told him what I was looking for he laughed and said, "Go back to your work. The men are fooling you. There is no such thing." All the men started laughing when I returned to the card room, and the foreman walked over to me and said, "You don't want to believe anything that these fellows tell you. They are like a bunch of monkeys, always thinking up fool stunts. The only thing that they never think about is their work." From that time on I was accepted as a member in good standing of the card room gang.

When I brought home my first pay I felt very important, and my mother allowed me to keep fifty cents. This was more money than I ever had before, so I promptly changed the fifty cent piece into nickels. How I swaggered around the Social District that night! After I had carefully looked and was sure that neither my older brothers nor my father were inside, I entered a saloon, strode to the bar, and ordered beer. The bartender, who was talking to a customer, did not glance at me but drew the glass of beer. When he put the glass of beer on the bar he looked at me, started laughing, and said, "Say, Sonny, who do you want this beer for?" I said, "I'm a working man, and I drink beer." The bartender replied, "Not if I know it. Run along now, and come back in a couple of years." As I retreated toward the door the bartender asked his customers if any of them knew me. One of them answered, "Sure, I know that fellow, he's the son of Henry Boucher. I think that he is going to get a kick in the pants when Henry hears that he went into a saloon." At this answer all of the men at the bar started laughing, and I found myself with plenty to worry about, for I knew that when my father heard of me going into a saloon he would be angry. Sure enough, two days later my father came home in a rage and said, "Henry, you are a big fellow now. Just because you work you think that you can get drunk. Well, I tell you that if I find you in a saloon I'll kick you all the way home."

But in spite of this I was determined to be a man, and as all the men in the card room chewed tobacco I bought a plug and tried chewing. It was a terrible taste, but I kept on chewing. Soon I swallowed some of the tobacco. Immediately my stomach started to turn over, and colored lights seemed to flash before my eyes. I was sick, very sick, and I sat on the floor groaning and wishing that chewing tobacco had never been invented. The second hand, seeing me sitting on the floor, ran over to me and asked, "What is the matter? Are you sick?" The other men ran over to me, but when they saw the tobacco juice that had started to dribble from the corner of my mouth, they knew why I was sick, and their laughter was long and loud. Knowing that I would soon recover they returned to their work, leaving me sitting on the floor. For weeks afterward, whenever a man came near me, he would hold a plug of tobacco in front of my face and offer me a chew. Upon my refusing the man would grin and say, "You'll never be a man until you are able to chew tobacco."

The work was not hard, and I enjoyed the companionship of the men in the card room. After I had worked there for a few months I was given a better job tending the finishers, and another young lad was hired to do my job. Then I had the pleasure of seeing someone else being the butt of all the jokes that the men played upon a newcomer. In the mills at the time working conditions were not as strict as they are now. A man had a lot of time to himself. There was very little piecework, and the young men were continually playing tricks on each other.

One of these tricks caused my discharge. One morning a fellow worker sneaked up behind me and hit me with a bunch of oily waste. When I looked around I saw the fellow, who had thrown the waste, enter the washroom. Looking around the card room I saw that the foreman was in his office, so I grabbed one of the fire pails hanging on the wall, carried it to a position in front of the washroom door, and waited there for the fellow to step out. The door started to open. I lifted the pail, and as the door swung wide I threw the water into the opening. I stood there laughing, holding the empty pail, waiting to see how my fellow worker liked his bath, when to my amazement through the door came the Superintendent. He was drenched from head to foot. Swearing and vowing that he would have revenge upon whoever threw the water, the Superintendent's glance fell upon me. I was standing there with a frightened look on my face. The Superintendent strode over to me and roared, "Did you throw that water?" I was unable to speak and could only nod yes. The Superintendent then said, "This is a hell of a room. You're fired. I should fire the whole crew. Get out of here before I lose my temper." He then strode down the room, still muttering, to let the foreman know just what he thought of the discipline in the card room. I took off my overalls, went to the office, and received my pay. When I arrived home and told my father what had happened, I received another lecture from him.

I then went in search of a job every morning. I landed one as a clerk in a grocery store within a week. The grocer was a deacon of a church and a very pious man, but he did not let his religious activities interfere with his method of doing business. During my first day's work he called me aside and said, "Henry, when you refill the sugar barrel I want you to put in one pound of this white sand to every twenty pounds of sugar. In this store the tobacco becomes too dry and loses weight so one of your duties is to add water to the tobacco. Make sure that you keep it damp. And when you are weighing meat be sure that you have your thumb on the scales. I am operating on such a close margin that I have to do these things in order to make a profit." My hours of labor were long, and the pay was but five dollars a week during the eighteen months that I worked for this public-spirited grocer.

Throughout 1913 and the first part of 1914 the mills were very slack, and the family had to live on my pay as my brothers and my father were without work most of the time. Although the family could not live on five dollars a week, the storekeeper of that period would allow a responsible family to run a bill. When the mills started in September, 1914 it seemed as if my father owed money to everyone in the city. With the mills running steadily my father, by allowing the family only the scantiest living, was able to pay most of the back bills within a few months.

I now left the grocery store and went to work as a doffer in the spinning room of the White mill. As this was a worsted mill, nearly all of the help in the spinning room were girls and women. After being employed here for a short while I found that it would be impossible for any girl or boy working here, to remain innocent of the facts of life, as sex was almost the only topic of conversation in the spinning room.

I did not work in the White mill very long. My brother found me a job as filling carrier in the Dunn Worsted Company. My duties were to carry yarn, used as filling, to the weavers. As I was in the weave room most of the time I learned to weave by watching the weavers work. Many times they would ask me to tend their looms while they went to talk to a fellow worker in another part of the room. The mill was running twenty-four hours a day, as orders were coming in from the warring European nations, and there wasn't enough experienced help to go around. After I had worked as a filling carrier for eight months I was given a loom, and they tried me out as a weaver. This was a swell job for a young man. Soon I was making $18 a week, and after paying $8 a week at home for board and room, I had $10 for myself. During the years 1915-1917 the mill was running day and night. The rate of pay had been raised many times until in 1917 I was making $40 a week. I was now paying $15 a week at home and had $25 a week for spending money. My father and my brothers were also making plenty of money.

After many a family argument my father decided to buy a new suit. His Sunday suit was ten years old and the blue cloth had faded so that its color was purple. But he thought that it was a sinful waste of money to buy a new suit while the cloth of the old suit held together. My mother threw away her old hat that she had had for many years. Until then she had replaced the hat's ribbon and the imitation flowers with new ones every spring. On the first Sunday that my father and mother wore their new clothes they went to High Mass as they wanted everyone to see them.

My father urged me to save some of the money that I was making, but I was having too good a time spending it. I bought myself four suits, four pairs of shoes, hats and many things that I had always wanted but could never afford, such as silk shirts, silk underwear, and a new Ford car. While I never was a drunk, my liquor bill would be about $8 a week. After the day's work I would meet my friends in the corner saloon, and there we would play cards and talk things over. It was wonderful—from a drab and dreary existence I was now able to live as formerly one of the foremen of the mill had lived. I did not have to eat soup, I could purchase steak. I did not have to live in a basement, I could pay the rent in a residential district. No matter what I spent, another week's pay was coming. My friends would gather at the saloon and then start out for a dance or a party. You did not have to worry about your job. No matter what you did, the boss would not dare fire you. It was seldom that I went to bed before two a.m. If you went to work in the morning with a big head, or even slightly drunk, the boss would overlook it, as the mill could not obtain enough help. During this period I was able to gratify my repressed desires with one long carousal.

In September, 1917 I was drafted for the army, and the night before I left my friends held a party for me. It was a wild party with everyone drinking, telling stories, and singing the French songs of Old Canada. The France Frenchmen that I knew gave me the names and addresses of either their families or their friends in France. The next morning all of my family was at the railroad station to wave good-bye to me. I was sent to Camp Dix, New Jersey, and after a few weeks' training I found myself on board a boat bound for France.

We landed at Brest, and I was assigned to the 107th regiment of the 77th Division as a replacement. When we arrived at the village, where my company was training, I was billeted in a French farm house. Being the only one in the company able to talk French I had a fine time as the other soldiers would pay me, with free drinks, to translate their desires to the inhabitants of the town. When the old French couple, whose house I was billeted in, learned that I was of French descent, nothing that they had was too good for me. They introduced me to all the inhabitants and to the mayor of the town. In the French newspapers there was an article that stated, "A million wild Indians were coming from America to fight the Germans." All of the French people asked me if they had landed, what they looked like, would they murder the French people if they were let loose, and would they scalp the Germans. The Frenchmen's knowledge of Indians was gained from the Wild West movies that they had seen. The soldiers of my company thought that this was too good an opportunity to miss, so four of them painted their faces, fashioned some Indian suits out of old clothes and with a blanket wrapped around them paid a visit to the mayor of the town. The mayor greeted them formally and held a party in his house with the "Indians" as the guests of honor. All of the inhabitants of the town attended the party. Whatever the "Indians" wanted was given them, for the French people had seen at the movies the massacre that ensued when Indians went on the warpath.

Shortly after this my regiment was ordered up to the lines where we participated in several battles. Although many of my friends were killed I came through without a scratch. When I was demobilized at the end of the war, I returned to Woonsocket.

After loafing around for about a week I went over to the Dunn Worsted Co. to see if I could have my old job back, but I was told that the mill was running on short time. Unable to obtain employment in the textile mills I went to work in the Woonsocket Rubber Co. as a trucker. This job only paid $22, but I was compensated in another way, for while working here I met the girl that later became my wife. In 1922 the mills started running full time, and I was able to obtain employment as a weaver in the Montrose mill. This mill was making a very high grade worsted cloth, and a weaver was able to make $35 a week.

Shortly after I started working in the Montrose mill I married Alice Deschamps, the French Canadian girl that I had met while working in the Woonsocket Rubber Co. I was 24 years old and Alice was 20. Two nights before the wedding my friends held a stag party for me. They hired a hall, and about one hundred men gathered there to celebrate my marriage. Father Didion, my pastor, who knew everything that happened in the parish, arrived at the hall early, and to the consternation of other guests he sat down and started eating. After the meal he made a short speech on the duties of a married man. He then proposed a toast to the young couple and showed that he was the soul of discretion by announcing that it was getting late and that he had some duties to attend to at the parish house. When he left everyone in the hall felt relieved, as most of the acts that they had hired in Boston were of the "striptease" type and it was not possible to have them perform while the good Father was in the hall.

There is one event that I'll always remember, and that is my wedding. I had on a morning suit, the first that I had ever worn. It was hired for the day. All of our friends were at the church, and the breakfast at the bride's house was a gay affair. We had a bartender to handle the liquor and a dance orchestra to play for the dancing. Late in the afternoon we left for New York City. I had been there before, but my wife Alice had never seen New York. What fun we had for the next two weeks exploring the city, and what stories we had to tell our friends when we returned.

After the honeymoon we returned to our jobs, I to the mill and Alice to her job in the rubber shop where she made $24 a week. After we had settled down I became ambitious for the first time in my life. We talked it over and figured out a budget by which we could save $20 every week. We planned to save this amount every week for the next twenty years, by which time we would be worth $20,000. Then we intended to buy a farm and spend the rest of our lives, in peace and quiet, never again to worry about a job, slack times, or the necessity to answer the mill bell. It was a beautiful dream, and we tried to make it a reality. On the second anniversary of our marriage we had $2,500 in the bank, $500 more than we had planned on. We were living in a comfortable and modern home in a residential district. The furniture was paid for, and we did not owe a cent to anyone. We were also the proud possessors of a Ford car that was nearly paid for.

That night we were very happy and proud of what we had accomplished in the two years since our marriage. Our friends gathered at our home, and we held a party. It was a gay party. Some of the time was spent in singing old songs and telling stories. Then all gathered around and started telling of the hardships that each of us went through in our childhood—how we had to wear our older brother's cast-off clothing that was so faded and patched that you could not tell what the original color was; how each of us longed for Sunday, as that was the only day on which we had meat for dinner. The life that we had lived as children was, in 1924, laughable, for all of us knew that conditions could never be like that again. How could we foresee the future? Everyone at the party was well-clothed, well-nourished, happy, willing to work for what they desired, and were working at good pay. Each one was planning to possess more of the necessities and the luxuries of life. One wanted an electric refrigerator, another a new car. Some were saving so that they might purchase a home or a business.

During our third year of married life, in 1925, a son was born to us. He was named Henry in honor of my father-in-law. A few months previous to the birth of our son my wife gave up her job in the factory, but as I had had a promotion to warp-starter and was making $50 a week we were able to continue saving $20 every week. The next year we became the parents of a daughter, whom we named Marie. From this time on I was unable to save $20 a week but put in the bank some money every payday. After the birth of our second son, Homer, in 1927, my wife became ill and needed medical attention. Because of this I was unable to save any money, for the doctor's bills used up whatever surplus money we had.

In 1928 work in the mills began to slacken, and I was laid off. After being out of work for two months I secured employment in the Saranac mill as a weaver. At this job I received $40 a week, but I believed that in a short time I would again find employment as a warp-starter. The next year conditions were worse, and I was without work for three months. My wife and I were not worried about the future, as we believed that the mills would be slack for only a short period, as they were in 1921. So we lived on what I made and did not touch the $3,500 that we had in the bank. I was without work for six months in 1930, and we were forced to use some of the money that we had saved. But I was in a better position than most of my friends who were buying houses and were unable to meet their payments. My brother Peter was caught in this condition, and as the bank was going to foreclose on his house I loaned him $500. I knew that he, a cutter in the rubber shop, making $70 a week, would be able to repay me as soon as his work picked up. Then without warning the rubber shop closed down and moved out of the city, throwing 1,500 people out of work. The next year, 1931, the bottom dropped out of everything, and we were forced to use up most of our savings. In only one way was I fortunate, and that was that I had no more doctor's bills to pay as my wife was well again. The bank foreclosed on my brother's house, and my $500 was gone. My father died in July, and after the funeral my mother came to live with us. She did not live long after my father but died in October, 1931. As neither my father nor mother believed in life insurance all of their children contributed to the cost of the funerals. I was unable to find work and spent the entire year hanging around the streets. By the end of 1931 my bank balance was less than $500 and was going down rapidly.

In September, 1932 I reached the end of my resources. I was desperate. With a wife and three children to support I was unable to find work of any kind. All of my friends were in the same predicament. Finally I had to go on relief, and what a relief that was! I shall always remember my experience while trying to get relief from the city. I went down to City Hall and registered at the Poor Department. After looking me up they gave me a pass to obtain food. But in order to receive the food I had to stand in line on Main Street with every passerby staring at me.

One day I stood in a line that blocked one side of Main Street for four hours before I received a small bag of flour and two pounds of dried peas. Of course my family was unable to live on what I received from the Poor Department, so I was continually moving to cheaper tenements until at last I was living in a basement on Social Street, the same type of tenement I was born in. The home that I had taken such pride in was broken up, and the fine furniture that my wife and I had worked for was sold to secondhand furniture dealers. It was not correct to say that I sold the furniture because the money that I received for it was so little that it was almost equivalent to giving it away. But my children had to have food and clothing. The rent had to be paid and the coal to be bought.

There was a soup kitchen on Social Street, and my son would go down there with a pail and bring home some soup. This helped out the small amount of food that I received from the Poor Department and kept my family from actual starvation. My family was very poor when I was a child, and when work in the mills was slack we would not have much to eat, but in Woonsocket never before was it necessary for anyone to have to go to a public soup kitchen in order not to starve.

In 1934 I obtained employment as a weaver in the Montrose mill. I worked steady the whole year except for a few weeks when the mill was closed by a strike. But working conditions had changed. They were as different as day and night from the working conditions of the 1920 to 1930 period. The pay had been greatly reduced, and the amount of work per man had been increased. I had been making $40 a week as a weaver operating two looms. Now I was operating six looms on the same material and only making $24 a week. I was lucky that I was working on fine worsted cloth because in some mills on coarser cloth, the weavers operated from eight to twenty-four looms for $24 a week. Apparently the only thing that a textile worker could rely upon in those times was that the mill owner would never suffer low profits as long as he could transfer the burden to his employees.

In 1935 I was again laid off, and the money that I had made in 1934 was soon used up. Then back to the relief I went. Since that time I have worked about six months in each year, and being unable to support my family when I am not working, I usually spend the rest of the year on the relief. The last place that I worked was in the Montrose as a weaver in the spring of 1938. I worked there for four months, but I knew that it would not last forever.

One morning I left my house, and as I entered the weave shop I could sense the tension that seemed to be in the air. The looms clattered, the men moved about. The belts and pulleys whirred. A typical weave room interior. But on this Friday morning there was something lacking. No one was talking, there was no laughter. Joseph Boyce, who worked next to me, did not raise his head from his work to call a greeting, nor did he ask me how I intended to spend the weekend as he was wont to do. Everyone was silently working, busy with their thoughts. For about a week past there had been rumors that the work in the mill was getting slack. Only three days ago six spinners were laid off, and the rumor was that eight weavers would lose their jobs this afternoon. I was, in length of service, one of the youngest weavers in the mill, and I believed that I would be one of the first to be laid off. But there was nothing sure about it. Sometimes an old hand, whom the boss disliked, was laid off and a newcomer kept. This uncertainty kept every weaver under a strain until they knew just who was to get the bounce. So they continued to work hard and silently until lunch time, for this was one day that no one wanted to make a mistake and have the foreman's attention called to him. While eating lunch the weavers could talk of nothing but who was to be laid off. While the newcomers believed that they would be the first to go, many of the old-timers remembered how they had spoiled yards of cloth and how displeased the boss had been with them. They wondered if he would remember the many times that he had bawled them out and take revenge by letting them go. So in this frame of mind the weavers started the afternoon shift.

This afternoon the foreman of the weave room did not walk around the room as he was accustomed to do, and it was nearly the close of the afternoon before he stepped from his office. Instantly the eyes of all the weavers were upon him, watching where he was going, and each man hoping the foreman would not come to him with the sad news. I saw the foreman turn to a weaver and start talking to him. They talked for a few minutes while everyone in the room watched. The foreman then turned away and approached another weaver. The first weaver spread his arms out wide in a gesture, and everyone then knew that the foreman was laying off help. All eyes then turned to the foreman, watching to see who was being laid off. I watched the slow progress of the foreman as he went from man to man, telling them the bad news. He was now at the next loom, and I prayed that I might be spared. But it was not to be, for the foreman slowly walked over to me and said, "You know what I have to say. I have a list of men who are to be laid off, and your name is on it. They are laying off in every room of the mill, and if more work don't come in the rest of the weavers will be out next week. This is no reflection upon your work which has been good, and I'll be glad to hire you back just as soon as the work picks up." I replied, "Well, I guess all the fellows here are in the same boat that I'm in. All of us are broke. This will mean plenty of hardship for my family. After eating good for the past five months, the first few meals of the relief canned corned beef is going to be hell for the kids. But thanks for your offer to rehire me when the work picks up. I'll certainly be glad to get back to work." The foreman then returned to his office, and the weavers gathered into a group asking each other what the boss said to them. The men who were laid off, now that the tension had been broken, began to joke and one said, "Will Johnny Ryan, the Director of Public Aid be glad to see me? Like hell he will. The last time I was on relief I had to haunt him in order to get any commodities. Every time he turned around I would be at his elbow asking for something." Another said, "This loafing is all right in some ways, but I'll always blame the last lay off for the twins my wife had." I said, "I wonder how long I'll have to wait for my unemployment compensation checks. The last time I had to wait ten weeks before I got the first one, and then the amount was wrong." And so for a few minutes they joked and talked of the future. They then returned to work.

My mind was not on my looms. I was thinking of the greatly lowered standard of living that my family would have to endure while I was out of work. I thought of my new radio that I was paying a dollar a week on. That would soon be taken back by the dealer. And then there was the dreadful ordeal of informing my wife and the children that I had been laid off. I knew that there would be no happiness or laughter in my home this night. How would I support my family on the six or seven dollars a week that I would receive from a relief? How long would I be without work this time? I stood there thinking these gloomy thoughts, not caring how my looms ran. What did I care now if a smash or dropped thread was made in the cloth? Let someone else worry about that. At bell time I made a bundle of my overalls and silently slipped out of the mill. I started walking home wishing that the road was twice as long so that I would not have to face my family so soon.

When I reached home my wife saw by the sorrowful look upon my face that something had gone wrong, and she asked, "What is the matter, Henry?" I replied, "The same old thing. I'm laid off and don't know when I'll go back." Across my wife's face an expression of fear flashed, but she quickly rallied and said, "Well, you can't help that, so stop looking as though you were at your own wake. We have been on relief before, and we're still alive so sit down and eat your supper. You'll feel better then." I sat down at the table but could eat very little. All this time the children, seated around the table, had been listening to the conversation and looking at me with wide, staring eyes. Only too well did they know what this meant: less food, no new clothes, no money to go to the movies, peeking through the window curtains when someone knocked upon the door to see if it was a bill collector, moving to a less desirable tenement. In short, misery for everyone in the family. After supper I was unable to stand the silence and gloom that seemed to settle over the house so I put on my coat and said, "Alice, I'm going down to the corner for a minute." My wife, knowing full well where I was going said, "Make sure you come home sober." So, leaving the house I hurriedly walked to "Fat's" saloon. In there, men would be talking upon every subject. There would also be jokes and laughter for a few hours. I could forget that my next pay would be the last one that I would receive for a long time.

The next day I applied for my unemployment compensation, and because of waiting for these checks I was unable to go on the relief for two months. By this time I was completely broke, so for the next few months we struggled along on the six dollars a week that I received from the relief. But week by week we were going deeper in debt for rent, electricity, and many other small bills. One morning a deputy sheriff handed me an eviction notice and departed. And there I sat in the kitchen, alone, forlorn, and in despair. It was the morning of November 25, just one month before Christmas, and in my hand I held the notice from the court to evacuate the tenement that I occupied. This was not the first eviction notice that I had ever received. During the past ten years, the deputy sheriffs had worn a path to my door delivering eviction notices, writs of attachment and liens on my pay. How could I break the news to my wife when she returned from a visit to a neighbor's house? Where could we go? When you are on relief and only receive six dollars a week it is impossible to support a family and pay rent. The landlords did not care to rent a tenement to families on relief as they could not be sure of their rent. So most of them were demanding their rent in advance. If I could find a tenement, where could I borrow the three dollars for the first week's rent? What a Christmas was in store for my children! As I sat there alone with my thoughts the door opened, and my wife walked in. Without talking I handed her the eviction notice. She knew what it was. She had seen many of them since 1930. Silently she laid it down and started to prepare dinner, each of us wondering where we could find a tenement.

A knock on the door. We looked at each other. What more trouble was coming to us? Good news had been absent from our lives for more than ten years. My wife slowly and listlessly walked to the door and opened it. There stood Adrian Bonin, with a broad smile upon his face and he said, "O boy, Henry, I have fine news for you. The boss wants you to come to work tomorrow morning. The mill got a big order. We'll work all winter." It seemed like a miracle. The house seemed brighter. Wide smiles appeared upon our faces. We started asking questions of Adrian. Who was the order for? What looms would I have? How does the yarn run? Which of the men were going back to work? Adrian answered as best he could and soon left. Dinner was forgotten, and my wife and I were still talking in an excited manner when our children came in for dinner. They sensed the jovial mood of my wife and myself, and when they heard the news they too forgot about dinner in thinking of the happiness that this news meant. Their father was going back to work. There would be new clothes for all and toys and presents at Christmas. After the children had gone to bed Alice and I sat up talking. We planned how we would spend my first week's pay to the best advantage. By paying a little each week on the old bills we would soon be out of debt. We would not have to move now for as soon as the landlord knew that I was working he would forget about his eviction. And if we needed money at Christmas we would easily borrow it from the small loan company. So in a happy frame of mind we went to bed.

The next morning I was at the mill gates an hour before bell time. There I found all of my fellow workers, and I joined in their conversation. Each asked the other what they had been doing during the lay off and what were they going to do with their first pay? There were predictions, laughingly made, that "Fat's" saloon would do a rushing business on pay night. But under all this gay jesting everyone of us knew that when the order was finished in a few months, we would again be laid off to tramp the streets while we collected our unemployment compensation checks, and then back on relief we would have to go until the mill started running full time again. We had gone through this routine many times in the past ten years, and each one of us knew that he would go through it many times in the future. But that knowledge could not dim our spirits today because we knew that while the mill operated we would be able to eat what we wanted, we could dress our families, and have a dollar left so that when meeting our fellow workers in "Fat's" saloon on Saturday night each one of us could stand up to the bar and pay for a round of beers.

Afterword

Rich as these life history narratives are in revealing the human condition of the earliest Franco-Americans, they are also significant historical documents. Their individual and concrete outlook accelerates the development of a new kind of Franco-American history, oriented to ordinary people and not to elite institutions. For too long we have relied on that monopoly of the written word held by newspapermen and priests, without also remembering that priests had careers to make and many a francophone journalist hoped to advance to a large-circulation Quebec daily newspaper. It is clear from these narratives, however, that ordinary Franco-Americans did not always think and behave as their leaders desired. Father Ouellette admitted that his Old Town parishioners did not emulate his reading of the French language press. Nor do Henry Boucher's mill town memories of male/female relationships indicate that Franco-American young people always followed their priests' advice when it came to relating to one another.

Rather, the discovery and publication of these life-history narratives, the earliest ones available to us, give us an opportunity to re-examine what we already know of the Franco-American experience. In particular, these personal life-histories allow us to substantiate, from the bottom up, what historians have discovered thus far about Franco-American life. Their memories and viewpoints also suggest answers to currently unanswered questions about the Franco-American past and provide signposts for the direction new research might take.

One theme of these life-history narratives is an ambivalence toward the French Canada left behind. In some narratives, there was no regret for leaving what the narrators remembered as unrelieved poverty and backwardness. That memory is most vivid in the account of the Ovide Morins of Old Town. They recalled deep snows requiring three weeks to dig out of and snowshoeing to church, children going barefoot even in winter, diets of bread and pork, and low wages. Worst of all, however, were the mean spiritedness and despair. Certainly, "conditions were very bad up there" and pay was low, but what galled Ovide Morin most was his employer's effort to get him to "do two days' work in one" in storing potatoes in the cellar until midnight after having harvested them from 4:00 A.M. until 6:00 P.M.[1] Or, again, the $2.00 annual salary of the middle-aged housekeeper was bad enough. Even worse was the hopelessness of having only one hat, "put *so carefully* in a tall hat box," and only one pair of old-fashioned shoes that "she wanted to keep as long as she lived."[2] As they recalled experiences such as those, most Franco-Americans in the 1930s would have agreed with Vital Martin of Old Town. "Yes, sir," he told the interviewer, "the world has improved very much since I lived in Canada."[3] For people such as these, the break with Canada was irrevocable. It was not a place to go back to.

Not all immigrants made such a clean break with Canada. Many came to "the States" temporarily. With their mill earnings they would return to the rural Canadian environment they preferred to the mill towns. The Manchester narratives, especially, show this coming and going between French Canada and French New England before settling down. The Manchester grandmother delighted in returning to the Quebec farms of uncles and aunts in the summers "when the mills were so hot that it was almost impossible to breathe inside them." She clearly loved and missed the farm animals and "Oh! the thick, yellow cream, the small, sweet strawberries of the fields, the raspberries, blueberries we had there."[4] What a pleasure it was for her to learn household arts like *catalogne*-making. For people like her, the mills of Manchester held little

Young boy leaves the Amoskeag Mfg Company at quitting time (6:00 PM), Manchester, New Hampshire, May 24, 1909.

appeal. One of Philippe Lemay's friends, like so many Franco-Americans that historians have spoken of, returned to Quebec to be a storekeeper, found a wife there, and returned to Manchester's mills.[5]

Of course, the Canada so badly remembered was no more backward or poor than many other places in late nineteenth century North America. The numerous abandoned farms of Yankee northern New England bear testimony to that. After fondly recalling his New Brunswick childhood, unemployed Old Town weaver Steve Comeau concluded that while people did not have the plumbing and electrical appliances of the 1930s when he was a boy, "we enjoyed ourselves just as much as people do now."[6] And, of course, had Comeau spent his boyhood in Old Town he probably would not have had such plumbing and electrical appliances either.

While the lure of a better standard of living in the United States caused them to tear up their Canadian roots, leaving

Canada was not always easy nor was it done without opposition. The long speech to the Manchester grandmother's father by the local Quebec storekeeper on the merits of not emigrating must have been repeated over and over again in nineteenth century Quebec. But leave they did, because "they were looking for a better place to live," as Steve Comeau put it, and there were not that many opportunities at home.[7]

In describing their journeys from Canada to "the States," they substantiate and make concrete what we have learned from the studies on "chain migration." Mike Pelletier's family came to Old Town from Rivière-du-Loup by covered wagon. The Morin family made the same journey by rail through Montreal and Danville Junction, Maine, to take over a farm owned by a cousin who had come earlier from Quebec. Nor are we surprised that Morin family members went on to Salem, Massachusetts, if we have read Ralph Vicero's research that the Salem population was increased by Quebecois from the Rivière-du-Loup region. The Morins could be met at the Salem train station by relatives and friends from "home." And, when Henry Boucher tells us that his parents were born in the Richelieu valley, we nod knowingly if we have read any of the studies on Woonsocket. That was where most Woonsocket Franco-Americans originated. There, too, the later immigrants were met at the train stations by friends and relatives who had immigrated earlier.

One after another, the narratives tell of similar journeys. Having carried a boatload of hay and grain from the St. Lawrence to Lake Champlain in 1881, Henri Lemay gave up his ambition to become a *pilote branche* and took the train to Manchester where he knew he could find work at higher pay in the mills. Alcide Savoie left Iberville, Quebec, to build summer cottages on Lake Champlain before moving on to a stonecutter's life in Barre, Vermont. The Lachance family was lured to Barre for the same reason from a failed farm in Chambly, not so far from Iberville, and at least one more Chambly neighbor joined them as a strikebreaker in 1922. Steve Comeau's train took him from New Brunswick to Greenville, Maine, for work in the woods before he moved on to the mills of Waterville and Old Town. In 1864, it took Philippe Lemay's family four days to go by train from St. Ephrem d'Upton, near Montreal, to Lowell, Massachusetts, with overnight lodgings in Sherbrooke, Island Pond, Vermont, Portland, and Boston. Even then, his mother was delayed several more days to give birth to another Lemay at Island Pond.[8] Philippe Lemay may have been one of the first to come to Manchester from the Montreal region, but because of "chain migration" he would be far from the last.

Just as most Franco-Americans came through "chain migration" to towns already inhabited by friends or relatives, most got jobs through a kind of "chain employment" in mills employing those same friends and relatives. "My older brother found a job for me in the card room of the Lippitt mill," admitted Henry Boucher in what was the typical experience of Franco-Americans. When he could not find the "left-handed monkey-wrench" during his first day on the job, that same brother explained the joke to him. Philippe Lemay may have gotten a job on his own at Manchester, but he found work in the mills for his son who, doubtless through his father's help, rose to be an overseer. Nor was the inability to speak English a handicap in this process of "chain employment." Even though he was bilingual, David Morin and the others found French to be the language of the workplace. When asked by a non-Francophone Salem foreman to bawl out a worker in French, he spoke in French all right, but he only pretended to reprimand her. He and other Old Town Franco-Americans highly regarded a local English lumberman, Gene Mann, who used French with his workers.[9]

In the new land, some found success. The two biggest events in his life, as Philippe Lemay recalled, were to become Manchester's first French spinner in 1875 and, in 1901, the city's first French overseer. When he applied for the overseer position, the superintendent looked "as if he had been struck by thunder and lightning. What! A Frenchman had the crust to think he could be an overseer." When Lemay got the job, the "Irish were mad clean through." They, it seemed, "were afraid that we had come to take their jobs away from them in the mills." "I, a Frenchman, had jumped over the heads of others who thought themselves the only ones entitled to the job of overseer. Here was a sin that could not be forgiven, and what was the world coming to, anyway?"[10] In the 1880s Henri Lemay left those same Manchester mills where he worked with his brothers, sisters, and parents, to becôme a clockmaker and jeweler.[11] In Old Town, Ovide Morin advanced from failed farmer, to woods worker, to bricklayer and contractor. His sons became prosperous candy merchants.[12]

Others had less success. Like Woonsocket's Henry Boucher, many Old Town Franco-Americans survived the Great Depression on relief or by working for the WPA. One reads these interviews wondering if anyone lived in Barre, Vermont, except those dying of silicosis, those about to get it, and the widows of earlier victims. Only Alcide Savoie struck an optimistic note when he reflected on his decision to become a stonecutter. "I can't say I'm sorry—not yet."[13] The "yet" had long since passed for the widow Lachance, whose stonecutter husband died young of silicosis. Having raised three daughters by running a boarding house, she worried that her youngest daughter would suffer a similar fate because her young man was sickly.

> He's a fine boy, . . . but I can't help but wish that it was someone else. Someone strong and well. I'd hate to think of her losing her husband as I did. Usually they are sick for a long time, months of sorrow and heartache. And afterwards, to be left alone with your children. . . . Sometimes I have wanted to speak to her, but then I think: she knows the story as well as I do. It will do no good. She will do what she wants, and it is her life to live.[14]

Another Barre French-Canadian stonecutter, dying of silicosis, postponed his inevitable hospitalization for fear of missing his son's graduation from high school.[15]

Whether they succeeded or failed, all participated in that basic conflict of whether to assimilate into anglophone America or to remain French in the tightly-knit ethnic communities of the *Petits Canadas*. Henry Boucher grew up speaking French at home, in school, and in the workplace. At the party on the eve of his departure for World War I, he and his friends from Woonsocket's Social District sang "the French songs of old Canada."[16] "We French people kept together and made our own good times," remembered Manchester's Henri Lemay.[17] Philippe Lemay recalled in great detail Manchester's numerous and varied *veillées canadiennes* with dances accompanied by fiddle and accordion, games such as *l'assiette tournante* and *chansons à répondre*. He hastened to add that in Canada "these home dances weren't allowed because our people believed that the devil himself was present as a cavalier wherever people danced. Stories of tragic happenings were told and made you shiver. Here, we . . . weren't afraid of the devil being in our homes if we conducted ourselves as decent people should."[18] Having "lived in several rooming houses," an unmarried Barre stonecutter "noticed that in the French houses the children are made to speak their native language more than in the Italian homes."[19] Old Town's David Morin made sure his children grew up speaking French as well as English, but that made him wonder if they were "French, or Americans, or Yankees? What is a Yankee, anyway? . . . Look back through the histories, and you'll see that the French were here just as soon as the English. . . . Have the descendants of the English any more right to be called Yankees than the descendants of the French?"[20]

Others took a different route. The Manchester grandmother struggled to learn English and use it in the home with her children because "it is of the greatest importance for a human being to adapt himself so as to be an integral part of the country where he lives his days." She recognized, however, her immigrant father's "feeling of loneliness, of being a stranger, of being nothing but an obscure cog in a gigantic machine" and that her mother's homesickness caused her to live "her life watching for the postman" bringing letters from Quebec.[21] Father Ouellette, the unquestioned leader of Old Town's French community, subscribed to Montreal's *Le Devoir* and Lewiston's *Le Messager*, referred to French-language volumes in his library on French North America, and made sure that French was taught in the parish school. Yet, he recognized that his parishioners were "unfortunately losing many of their racial characteristics . . . America is the great melting pot. All races are poured into it to emerge as one."[22] Some of his parishioners changed their names. Magloire ("Mike") Pelletier became Mitchell Pelkey, but his wife remained on the voter registration rolls as a Pelletier. Alex Lavoie became a Leavitt. William Green had found that Americans just could not spell Grenier, and Frank Wedge had had the same trouble with Aucoin.[23]

In their remembrances of the grinding poverty but sweet values of the French Canada left behind, of the varied paths of "chain migration," of the "chain employment" into the workplace, of success or failure, of acculturation or the retention of linguistic and ethnic loyalty, these life-history narratives make concrete the major themes of the Franco-American past as we now know it. At the same time, these narratives also suggest answers to those questions which continue to puzzle the historians of Franco-Americans: how do we explain the seeming slowness of Franco-Americans to participate in the trade union movement, and why was it that Franco-Americans have had less impact on New England politics than have such later arriving immigrants as Italian Americans and Greek Americans?

An interview with an Italian American granite cutter in Barre suggests that Franco-American workers were every bit as opposed to trade unions as the historical literature has assumed. For this cutter, the French were as bad as the "crackers" he had worked with in Georgia. "You can't organize them, either. I tried it. I tried to show them how the union would increase their pay. They wouldn't listen. They're too scared—and stupid." He remembered that the strike of 1922 was broken by strikebreakers brought in from nearby Quebec.[24] That is the stock view of anti-union Franco-Americans, a view that goes back at least to the 1881 characterization of them by Carroll Wright, director of Massachusetts' Bureau of Statistics of Labor, as "the Chinese of the Eastern States." "Docility is one of his most marked traits," William MacDonald could write of the Franco-American in 1898. "He is not over-energetic or ambitious. His main concern is to make a living for himself and his family, and, if that seems to have been attained, he is little troubled by restless eagerness to be doing something higher than that at which he is at present engaged. Above all, he is reluctant, as compared to the Irish, to join labor unions and is loath to strike."[25] Franco-Americans were, in short, docile workers. They followed their Church's lead in opposing, first, the Knights of Labor and, then, the American Federation of Labor. That reputation made them sought after by New England textile manufacturers of all sorts.

Yet, other Barre interviews indicate a different understanding of Franco-American views of trade unions. During the 1922 strike Mrs. Lachance's husband had been a good union man and had gone on strike. On the other hand one of his childhood friends from Chambly found work as a strikebreaker. "Can you blame him for accepting it?" asked widow Lachance. "I don't. He'd never worked in granite. . . . He came for the work, for money to keep his family together. . . . I don't blame him. . . . But I know he's a union man now, and a good one."[26] A Franco-American stonecutter, who also had followed his union out on strike, was equally tolerant. "The ones that stuck to the sheds and are still working feel different about [striking] now. I'll bet you couldn't get one of them to go now to some other granite area as a strikebreaker, not for twice the money they're earning. Lots of them are still ashamed of what they did. They don't even want to speak about it."[27]

It would seem foolhardy to make too much of Barre as a model. After all, Barre was too small a city, its Franco-American population too small a minority, its industry too atypical of Franco-American communities, and the evidence too fragmentary to provide any generalizations for trade unionism in New England's textile centers, the more typical setting for Franco-American life. Yet, in some ways, these very weaknesses suggest, in microcosm, answers to understanding that larger universe of the Franco-American trade union experience in the New England textile centers.

These narratives suggest that Franco-Americans came to Barre around 1900 for the same reasons they went elsewhere, to find jobs and escape the poverty of Quebec. They brought with them *la foi, la langue, et les moeurs* that other Franco-Americans brought in their intellectual baggage and, according to the narratives, they at least maintained *la langue* in the home. By 1922 established Franco-American granite workers struck with their fellow workers, while Franco-American newcomers scabbed. By 1930 Franco-Americans were in leadership positions in unions diminished in membership after the strike.

By the end of the 1930s, thanks to the Great Depression and the New Deal ethos, Barre Franco-Americans, like other workers, were almost totally unionized.

One might conclude that two factors account for this remarkably rapid unionization of Barre's Franco-Americans. One factor was cultural, the prior existence in Barre of radical European-born trade unionists and socialists who acted as mentors for the newly arrived Franco-American workers. Their initial small numbers and the absence of a French language parish, which elsewhere fostered ethnic exclusivity and solidarity, encouraged Franco-Americans to follow the European-born leadership. Another factor was social. The trade unionist solutions offered by the European-born mentors made sense to the Franco-American newcomers because of the conditions of the workplace. The first Franco-Americans arrived at the advent of the rising incidence of silicosis. Within twenty years they were presented with post-World War I pay cuts combined with longer work weeks. Within another ten or fifteen years they had experienced the economic hardships of the Great Depression. Under these changing working conditions, moreover, male heads of households, unlike their counterparts in the female-employing textile centers, had to provide the sole support for their families. In short, Barre Franco-Americans, like people elsewhere, had to learn to be working class trade unionists. They learned, like people elsewhere, from mentors teaching in an environment where what was taught was related to real life.

Readers familiar with the work of E.P. Thompson, George Rudé, and Eric Hobsbawm on "the making of the working class" in Europe and Herbert Gutman's application of their work to the American scene will not find this explanation particularly original.[28] The problem is, if this analysis is accurate for Barre Franco-Americans, why is it not applicable to Franco-Americans generally? They did, after all, remain hostile to trade unionism until very late.

The uniqueness of the Franco-American experience suggests an answer to this question. Unlike other immigrants to the United States, Franco-Americans came in one tidal wave almost exclusively into but one industry, textiles, in but one region, New England. Even in that region, they came not to the major urban centers, like Boston, but to the small and medium-sized cities of specific areas—the Merrimack, Blackstone, Quinebaug, and Connecticut River valleys, southeastern Massachusetts, and southern Maine.

The regional, indeed sub-regional, development within a single industry provided cultural and social factors, different from those in Barre, which impeded rather than fostered a working class or trade union consciousness. Much has been said already of the cultural factor. Small cities, such as Lewiston, Biddeford, Lowell, Fall River, and Holyoke, developed *Petits Canadas*, with their francophone parishes and parish schools and newspapers, similar to those already described in Manchester and Woonsocket. With "chain migration" and "chain employment", these *Petits Canadas* reinforced the bonds of kin and ethnicity. Henry Boucher's experience was typical of Franco-Americans elsewhere in textile manufacturing in demonstrating that kinship and ethnic networks did work for awhile. He got not one but several jobs through his brothers who also taught him the ropes. In turn, he helped them out when they needed it. Boucher's testimony bears out what we have learned from Tamara Hareven's study of Manchester.[29] Family and ethnic networks accomplished much of what people came later to expect from trade unions. These networks found jobs for their members, taught work routines to newly employed members, and covered for older members who could not keep up. They informally set the speed of work, found housing, and formed both formal and informal mutual aid arrangements to tide over members in hard times and to provide for old age.

The social factor—the one-industry reliance on textiles—gave a particular twist to the cultural factor of Franco-American ethnicity and added another dimension to the problem of Franco-Americans and trade unionism. Unfortunately for them, Franco-Americans arrived when the New England textile industry was at its peak. They spent their working lives as it went into decline. One can see this especially in spinning capacity, which rose steadily from over eight million spindles in 1880 to 18 million spindles in 1920 only to plummet to four million spindles in 1940. In contrast, the spinning capacity of Southern mills passed New England's capacity by 1925 and held steady at 17-18 million spindles.[30] With each passing year, then, the New England mills and their machines increasingly became museum pieces, compared to the newer, more efficient mills and machines in the South.

This peak and decline of the textile industry meant that the Irish, Scottish, and Yankee predecessors of the Franco-Americans, rather than serving as mentors as in Barre, were competitors both in the workplace and the community. Philippe Lemay had nearly total recall of the death of Jean-Baptiste Blanchette at the hands of the Irish, as if it happened yesterday rather than nearly fifty years earlier. The scorn and hatred which greeted his promotions were repeated in the lives of Franco-Americans everywhere. Nor was the *Sentinelliste* controversy of Woonsocket the only clash between Irish bishops and Franco-American parishioners. Less dramatic conflicts occurred in Fall River (1886), Danielson, Connecticut (1895-1897), North Brookfield, Massachusetts (1899-1904), and Maine's corporation sole controversy (1906-1914). The Irish were attracted to trade unionism early on, but their rivalry in the community prevented them from being mentors for Franco-Americans.

The workplace itself combined with Franco-American culture to impede unionism. While men were the breadwinners in Barre, entire families had to work to make ends meet in textiles. Unlike the granite industry, the textile industry was built with the labor of women. Nearly 70% of the female textile workers in the New England states, except in Vermont, were Franco-American in 1900. Moreover, as Tamara Hareven has told us, Franco-American women divided their lives between the "industrial time" of working in the mills and the "family time" of raising children. Because women divided their lives that way, they were hard to organize. There surely were exceptions, as Daniel J. Walkowitz discovered in Cohoes.[31] There, "widows"—older, never married or widowed principal breadwinners—assumed leadership positions in the labor struggles of the 1880s. For the most part, however, the textile industry employed such a high proportion of women that it was hard to organize. Cotton textiles, with the highest proportion of women workers, were the most difficult of all.

The trouble with understanding the attitudes of Franco-Americans toward trade unionism is due, in large part, to the fact that they were so visible in the difficult-to-organize textile industry and so invisible in other industries. Moreover, kinship and ethnicity initially facilitated satisfactory work rules and employment while fostering a distrust of potential trade union mentors. Had the social conditions of the textile industry been different, however, kinship and ethnicity might just as easily have prepared Franco-Americans for other group loyalties, such as trade unionism.

By the early twentieth century, however, the decline of the New England textile industry increasingly demonstrated that kinship and ethnic networks could no longer maintain satisfactory wages, hours, and working conditions. That decline turned textile workers of every ethnic group to trade unionism. Franco-Americans did participate in such strikes as that of Fall River (1904), Lawrence (1912), and throughout New England (1922). Gary Gerstle's 1982 dissertation, described earlier in the introduction to Woonsocket, demonstrates how dramatic this shift to unionism could be. The Barre life-history narratives show that Franco-Americans could quickly become unionists outside of the textile industry if they had mentors and a weak ethnic community. Gerstle confirms that the same thing could happen in a strong ethnic community in the textile industry, if that community had become fractured, if effective mentors presented themselves, and if the social conditions of the textile industry changed appropriately. What is needed now are more studies of a quality equal to those of Walkowitz, Hareven, and Gerstle. Particularly useful might be studies of Franco-Americans in the pulp and paper industry and its cities.

There still remains that other question: considering their numbers, why have Franco-Americans had so little impact on New England politics? The question is frequently asked, but seldom studied. The many books on the currently fashionable ethnic factor in politics are replete with references to Italian Americans, Black Americans, Irish Americans, Hispanic

Americans, and Greek Americans, but one can search their indices in vain for references to Franco-Americans.

Most writers on Franco-American politics make similar points.[32] In presidential elections, New England Franco-Americans divided their loyalties fairly evenly between Republicans and Democrats from 1892 until 1928. In 1928, Alfred E. Smith's Catholic faith took Franco-Americans with him, and their shift to the Democratic column was reinforced and made permanent by Franklin D. Roosevelt's New Deal. The Eisenhower presidency brought many Franco-Americans back to the Republican fold. They returned to the Democrats only with another Catholic, John F. Kennedy. Franco-Americans have remained Democratic stalwarts ever since.

The initial divided loyalties in presidential politics carried over into state and local politics, but in different ways in different states. Upon their arrival in "the States," Franco-Americans found local Democratic parties controlled by the Irish and local Republican ones in the hands of Yankees. In states like Rhode Island where Franco-Americans perceived that the greatest threat to their interests came from the Irish, more became Republicans than Democrats. In other states like New Hampshire and Maine where the greatest perceived threat came from Yankees, Franco-Americans were more likely to favor Democrats, but with many defections to the Republicans. Since the New Deal, however, Franco-Americans throughout New England have voted solidly Democratic at every political level.

This division of political loyalties is helpful in explaining the low impact of Franco-Americans on New England politics until the end of the 1920s, but it provides little guidance for the period after that time. The fact is that from the 1920s to the present, Franco-Americans have comprised 20-25% of the population of Maine, New Hampshire, Massachusetts, and Rhode Island. Among these states, however, Rhode Island stands alone in electing Franco-Americans to high office. In addition to its two Franco-American governors, both Republicans, it has elected a U.S. Senator and, since the 1920s, one of the state's two members of Congress. While New Hampshire's current Franco-American Congressman has been preceded by two others, neither Maine nor Massachusetts currently has a Franco-American member of Congress. Maine, with Jewish American and Armenian American Senators and a Greek American member of Congress, has yet to elect a Franco-American governor, senator, or member of Congress in this century. Only in city councils and state legislatures have Franco-Americans ever achieved political power commensurate with their proportion of the total population.

Some particularly peculiar elections stand out in the Franco-American political record. In 1956, Lewiston's overwhelmingly Franco-American population gave a majority to a Yankee candidate for Congress over a Franco-American. One might explain that by the fact that the Yankee was from Lewiston and was a Democrat. A decade and a half later, however, Lewiston voters, who customarily gave a 7-1 majority for any Democratic candidate, gave a Democratic Franco-American candidate for Congress only a 2-1 majority over his Jewish American Republican rival. In 1960, Manchester's 50% Franco-American population gave John F. Kennedy's candidacy a 12,000 majority while giving a 700 vote majority to the Republican Yankee candidate for governor over a Democratic Franco-American candidate. In Salem, Massachusetts, with an ethnic population nearly equal to the 45% of Irish Americans, Franco-Americans have never elected a mayor and rarely elected as many members to the city council as have the Irish.

In seeking to explain this lack of political success, scholars have invariably fallen back on arguments of "national character." The Franco-Americans are simply a people of apolitical rural origins, jealous of one another, "docile", emotional, individualistic, and mistrustful of other ethnic groups. Of course, these "characteristics" cannot be substantiated except by the most fragmentary anecdotal evidence. Moreover, most of these "characteristics" could be and have been attached to any other ethnic group. Try them, for example, for the politically astute Irish Americans. In short, "national character" simply will not do to explain Franco-American political involvement.

Again, our life-history narratives offer some suggestions. The rural Quebecois were hardly apolitical, if the Manchester grandmother was any judge. "You know how Canadians love politics; some say they play politics *du jour de l'an à la St. Syl-*

vestre."[33] That statement was immediately followed, however, by the observation that her father never became naturalized, while her husband was one of Manchester's first Franco-American citizens. If Quebecois were active politically in Quebec and under-active in the United States, their failure to become American citizens may be a major explanation for not establishing a greater political presence in the United States. Philippe Lemay suggested as much when he seemed to complain unduly that the first Franco-Americans "didn't like to become citizens and feared it for more than one reason. They couldn't speak English, and that, let me tell you, was a big handicap. They were afraid of war and might be drafted. Most of them were still taxpayers in the province of Quebec and the different places from which they came, and they felt that they couldn't pay taxes here too. Most of them hadn't come here to stay. What they wanted most was to go back to their Canadian farms with the money earned in the textile mills. So they kept putting off taking out naturalization papers." Lemay added that "able" Franco-American leaders "preached Americanization" and citizenship "as a duty to ourselves as well as to the country." He appeared to take comfort that "naturalization increased," but he did not trumpet its success as he praised other Franco-American accomplishments.[34] David Morin of Old Town could applaud the deportation of French Canadians. "Serves them right if they don't want to be citizens."[35]

These protestations about the need for naturalization are confirmed by much of the Franco-American literature through the early twentieth century. Typical of these were the thumbnail biographies in the frequent directories of the *Guide officiel des Franco-Americains*. An appropriate example would be that of Manchester's Henri Lemay:

> HENRI-I. LEMAY, bijoutier, né à Ste-Croix de Lotbinière, de Joseph et de Elèonore Parent; marié avec Mlle Emelda Rivard; membre des soc. F.-A.; *propriètaire et votant* (emphasis added).

As one reads page after page of such biographies, one is initially amused by this inclusion of information on property ownership and voting. Then one begins to consider why such information was included in edition after edition into the 1940s unless the absence of property ownership and voting was a problem.

At this point there is no answer to that question, because we do not have a very clear picture of the extent of naturalization and voter registration among the total Franco-American population in any place at any time. Nor do we know how Franco-American naturalization compares with that of other ethnic groups in New England. So far studies have looked mainly at the political participation or silence of Franco-American populations rather than that of Franco-American voters. We may find that Franco-Americans were simply slower than rival ethnic groups to become citizens, and that fact may help explain the low impact of Franco-Americans on politics.

Over time, the problem of naturalization would go away as the *Petits Canadas* came to include second and third-generation Franco-Americans who would have citizenship by place of birth. Even in this regard, these life history narratives provide some instruction. In explaining why Franco-Americans were slow to form fraternal organizations, Mike Pelletier of Old Town commented, "After a man worked fifteen hours a day about all he felt like joining was a mattress."[36] What was true for Old Town would be even more true for the Manchester and Woonsocket textile mill workers whose survival, even after hours were shortened, depended on entire families working.

This and other evidence would indicate that work in the declining and increasingly exploitive cotton textile industry, the workplace most common to the Franco-American experience, would impede the education and social mobility necessary to create Franco-American political leadership. Quebec priests, newspapermen, teachers, and doctors followed Quebec mill workers into the *Petits Canadas.* They were not followed, however, by that most political of all professions, the law. Franco-American mill workers could rise, without much education, to become shopkeepers. It was much more difficult to become lawyers. If the participation of Franco-Americans in politics was low in proportion to their numbers, it was nothing compared to their participation in the legal profession, the breeding ground of political leadership. Figures for Biddeford and Lewiston, from the *Guide Officiel* and the *Maine Register* of the 1920s and 1930s, demonstrate this very well. The populations of those cities in those years were 60-80% Franco-American. In those same years, the number of Biddeford's Franco-American attorneys rose from five out of the city's total of 21 in 1922 to seven out of the city's total of 30 in 1939. The percentage of Franco-American attorneys, however, remained at 23%. In the same period, Lewiston's Franco-American attorneys rose from five out of 39 in 1922 to 11 out of 50 in 1939, making the percentage rise from 12% to 22%. By that time, attorneys were law school-trained, and the law school of choice for Biddeford and Lewiston Franco-Americans was Boston University Law School. In all likelihood, the development of a Franco-American legal profession in Maine had to await the rise of the publicly-funded University of Maine School of Law in the 1960s. One would probably find a similar pattern in other New England states. In short, the initial absence of large numbers of Franco-American citizens and the later dearth of Franco-American lawyers do more to explain the failure to acquire an appropriate political power than all the so-called "national characteristics."

Initially sustained by ethnic solidarity and textile mill work, then, Franco-Americans came to be entrapped by both. Had they only arrived earlier during the rise of the textile industry or had they been more dispersed among other industries on the rise, the story of Franco-Americans might have been different. Ultimately, the textile industry's low wage scales forced entire families to work. In turn, that prevented Franco-Americans from receiving the educational and social opportunities enjoyed by so many other ethnic Americans. That lack of educational and social opportunity, rather than "national characteristics," is the chief explanation for the Franco-American record in politics and trade union or business success. Unfortunately, adequate educational and social opportunity has yet to come to many of New England's Franco-American textile "ghost-towns."

In short, these life-history narratives point to a history of Franco-Americans that is only now beginning to be written. The authors of these narratives indicate that they left behind, without regret, a Canada made familiar to us by Louis Hémon's novel, *Maria Chapdelaine*. Thanks to that oral tradition, their descendants wrongly assumed that Canada remained backward and rural. Once in the United States their principal concerns were not erecting parish churches, founding newspapers, and arguing ideological disputes. Instead, their chief interests were in growing up, getting and keeping a job, making the conditions of that job bearable, finding life companions, and seeing that their children would have better opportunities than they did. In accomplishing these ordinary, but vital life goals they were ambivalent between wishing to preserve their French traditions and language and deciding to assimilate. Their unique situation in the *Petits Canadas* of declining textile centers prevented them from achieving the political and social success one might have expected. It is to these concerns that the historians of Franco-Americans need to turn.

NOTES

[1] Page 60

[2] Page 61

[3] Page 93

[4] Page 40

[5] Page 28

[6] Page 54

[7] Pages 38-40 and 55-56

[8] Pages 16-17, 43, 56-57, 110-112, and 114

[9] Pages 17, 20, 62, 69, and 127-128

[10] Pages 19-20

[11] Page 45

[12] Pages 58-62

[13] Page 114

[14] Page 111

[15] Page 117

[16] Pages 126-132

[17] Page 44

[18] Pages 28-30

[19] Page 109

[20] Page 72

[21] Pages 40-42

[22] Pages 94-95

[23] Pages 88, 97, and 101

[24] Library of Congress, Manuscript Division, WPA Federal Writers' Project, Folklore Project-Life Histories, Vermont, Roaldus Richmond, "Stonecutter and Wife," p. 3.

[25] William MacDonald, "The French Canadians in New England," *Quarterly Journal of Economics*, 12, No. 3 (April, 1898), p. 245 Carroll Wright in *Thirteenth Annual Report* (1928) of the Massachusetts Bureau of Statistics of Labor.

[26] Pages 112-113

[27] Page 108

[28] See especially, Edward P. Thompson, *Making of the English Working Class* (London, 1963); George Rudé, *The Crowd in History* (New York, 1964); Rudé and Eric J. Hobsbawm, *Captain Swing* (New York, 1968); Hobsbawm, *Labouring Men* (London, 1963) and *Primitive Rebels and Social Bandits* (Manchester, 1959).

²⁹ Tamara K. Hareven, *Family Time and Industrial Time* (Cambridge, 1982).

³⁰ Steve Dunwell, *The Run of the Mill* (Boston, 1978), p. 157 especially.

³¹ Daniel J. Walkowitz, *Worker City, Company Town: Iron and Cotton Protest in Troy and Cohoes, New York, 1855-1884* (Urbana, 1978).

³² Most helpful to the following account were: David B. Walker, "The Presidential Politics of the Franco-Americans," *Canadian Journal of Economics and Political Science*, 28 (August, 1982), 353-363; Duane Lockard, *New England State Politics* (Princeton, 1959); Ronald A. Petrin, "Culture, Community, and Politics: French Canadians in Massachusetts, 1885-1915" in Claire Quintal (ed.), *The Little Canadas of New England* (Worcester, 1983), pp. 66-83; Patrick T. Conley, "Ethnic Politics in Rhode Island: The Case of the Franco-Americans" in Marcel P. Fortin (ed.), *Woonsocket, R.I.: The Americanization of a Foreign City* (Woonsocket, 1981), pp. 11-13; Norman Sepenuk, "A Profile of Franco-American Political Attitudes in New England" in Madeline Giguere (ed.), *A Franco-American Overview. Volume 3. New England (Part One)* (Cambridge, 1981), pp. 213-234; Harold R. Cox, "The French Canadian Ethnic Factor in Maine Politics" (Master of Arts Thesis, University of Maine at Orono, 1972); Michael J. Guignard, "The Franco-Americans: The Relationships Between Ethnic Identification and Political Behavior" (Bowdoin College Honors Thesis, 1969).

³³ Page 42

³⁴ Pages 24-25

³⁵ Pages 71-72

³⁶ Page 75